Nouns

- Nouns are the names for people, places, and things.

- A **proper noun** is the name of a particular person, place, or thing.

- A **common noun** is any noun that is not a proper noun.

- A **concrete noun** is something you can see, hear, smell, or touch.
- Concrete nouns are a type of common noun.

- An **abstract noun** is a noun (such as an idea, feeling, or event) that cannot be experienced through the five senses.

- Abstract nouns are a type of common noun.

Prepositions

- Prepositions relate one noun or pronoun to another.
- Examples include "to," "from," and "around."

Conjunctions

- A conjunction is used to join parts of a sentence.
- Examples include "and," "but," and "so."

Adjectives

- Adjectives describe a noun or a pronoun.
- Types of adjective include **comparatives** and **superlatives**, and **possessive adjectives**.

Adverbs

- Adverbs describe verbs.
- Usually, adverbs describe how, where, when, or how often something happens.

Verbs

- Verbs tell you what a person or a thing does or is.
- A verb can describe an action, an event, a state, or a change.
- The verb can take place in the past, present, or future.

Past
- Simple Past
- Past Continuous

Present
- Simple Present
- Present Continuous

Future
- Simple Future
- Future Continuous

Pronouns

- Pronouns are the little words used to replace nouns.
- Different pronouns are used for the subject and the object of a sentence. Pronouns can be singular or plural.

Singular Pronouns

I (Subject)

me (Object)

you (Subject)

you (Object)

he (S)   she (S)   it (S)
him (O)   her (O)   it (O)

Plural Pronouns

we (Subject)

us (Object)

you (Subject)

you (Object)

they (Subject)

them (Object)

Aa Bb Cc Dd Ee Ff Gg Hh Ii Jj Kk Ll Mm
Nn Oo Pp Qq Rr Ss Tt Uu Vv Ww Xx Yy Zz

‹age› ‹ege›

col lege
___ ___

priv i lege
___ ___

al lege
___ ___

man age
___ ___

cot tage
___ ___

vil lage
___ ___

mes sage
___ ___

ad van tage
___ ___

dam age
___ ___

her i tage
___ ___

av er age
___ ___

sav age
___ ___

cour age
___ ___

wreck age
___ ___

saus age
___ ___

lan guage
___ ___

or phan age
___ ___

mar riage
___ ___

Match the words in the spelling list to the descriptions below.

a very small town in the country
___

a place where older students go to study
___

to succeed in doing something difficult
___

a small house in the countryside
___

to say something is true, but have no proof
___

a special advantage only given to a few people
___

very violent or cruel
___

traditional things we value from the past
___

being usual or ordinary
___

to cause harm to something or someone
___

something that makes you more likely to succeed
___

information sent from one person to another
___

a wedding ceremony
___

a place where children who have no parents live
___

the use of words to communicate
___

a small tube of skin stuffed with meat and herbs
___

the remains of something destroyed in an accident
___

another word for bravery
___

Dictation: ‹age› ‹ege›

1. _____

_____

2. _____

_____

3. _____

_____

Complete these words by writing in the missing letters.

c _ k _

s _ _ l

n _ _ _ t

h i p _ _

m _ _ i c

b _ b _

k _ _ _ s

_ _ l a n d

t o m a t _ _ s

f _ _ _ y

l o a _ _ _

c a _ _ l e

p _ _ _ _ l s

w _ _ _ m s

h o r _ _

_ _ _ _ c h e s

Identify the subject; then parse the sentence and the verb.

The terrible hurricane severely damaged the cottages and houses in the village.

singular
plural

1st person
2nd person
3rd person

past
present
future

simple
continuous

3

Parts of Speech and Parsing

Nouns

Which parts of speech are these? Write the name for each one next to its description and underline it in the appropriate color.

Doing words that can describe the past, present, or future: _____

Names of people, places, dates, or things: _____

Words that describe nouns and pronouns: _____

Words that describe verbs: _____

Small words that take the place of nouns: _____

Words that join parts of a sentence together: _____

Words that relate one noun or pronoun with another: _____

Adjectives

Pronouns

Parse these sentences, identifying the parts of speech and underlining them in the appropriate color.

We live in a pretty thatched cottage near the village school.

The yellow submarine dived gracefully under the waves and

disappeared from view.

Zack's grandma had a big party on her eightieth birthday.

Verbs

Adverbs

Complete the sentences by writing an appropriate word in each space.

pronoun   _adjective_   _adjective_

_____ knitted me a _____ , _____ , and

adjective   _noun_

_____ scarf for my _____ .

adjective   _verb_   _preposition_

The _____ mouse _____ hurriedly _____

conjunction   _noun_

the hedge _____ into the _____ .

Prepositions

adjective   _adjective_

The _____ tree had a _____ crop of

noun

_____ this year.

Conjunctions

4

Write a sentence for each of the spelling words listed below.

change _____

_____

strange _____

_____

challenge _____

_____

orange _____

_____

plunge _____

_____

sponge _____

_____

exchange _____

_____

arrange _____

_____

lounge _____

_____

fringe _____

_____

revenge _____

_____

cringe _____

_____

‹nge›

change
_____
strange
_____
chal lenge
_____ _____
or ange
_____
plunge
_____
sponge
_____
ex change
_____ _____
ar range
_____
lounge
_____
fringe
_____
re venge
_____ _____
cringe
_____
sy ringe
_____ _____
a venge
_____ _____
twinge
_____
singe
_____
scav enge
_____ _____
in ter change
____ ____ ____

Dictation: ‹nge›

1. _____

_____

2. _____

_____

3. _____

_____

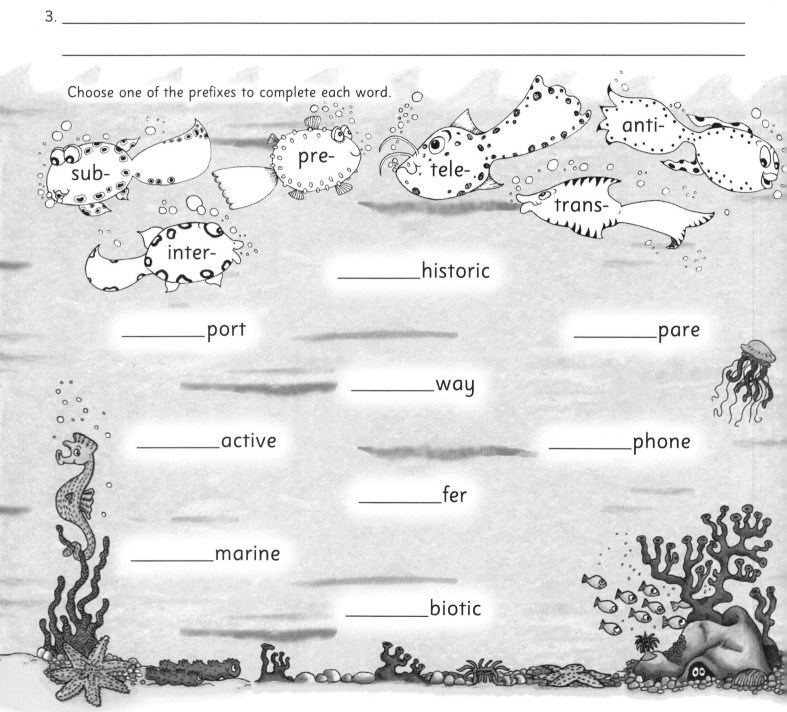

Choose one of the prefixes to complete each word.

sub- pre- tele- anti- trans- inter-

_____historic

_____port

_____pare

_____way

_____active

_____phone

_____fer

_____marine

_____biotic

Identify the subject; then parse the sentence and the verb.

The brave lifeguard plunges fearlessly into the choppy waters.

singular plural 1st person 2nd person 3rd person past present future simple continuous

6

One Word – Different Parts of Speech

These words can be different parts of speech, depending on how they are used. Write sentences for each word, using the parts of speech indicated, and underline that word in the appropriate color each time.

shower

noun _____

_____

verb _____

Nouns

Japanese

noun _____

_____

adjective _____

Adjectives

clean

adjective _____

_____

verb _____

Pronouns

Verbs

hard

adjective _____

_____

adverb _____

Adverbs

color

noun _____

_____

verb _____

_____

adjective _____

Prepositions

Conjunctions

7

dis tance

_____

ad vance

_____

bal ance

_____

en trance

_____

chance

_____

ac cep tance

_____

ad mit tance

_____

an noy ance

_____

as sis tance

_____

clear ance

_____

dis turb ance

_____

fra grance

_____

al le giance

_____

guid ance

_____

nui sance

_____

hin drance

_____

ir rel e vance

_____

ac quain tance

_____

Trace over the dotted letters. Then use the starting dots to practice writing ‹-ance›.

ance

Which of the spelling list words come from these root words?

to clear _____

to guide _____

to admit _____

fragrant _____

to annoy _____

to hinder _____

to accept _____

to disturb _____

to assist _____

to acquaint _____

relevant _____

Make nouns from these root verbs by adding the suffix ‹-ance›.

to avoid _____

to deliver _____

to utter _____

to allow _____

to endure _____

to insure _____

Dictation: ‹-ance›

1. _____

_____

2. _____

_____

3. _____

_____

Write two sentences for each word, using the parts of speech indicated.

puzzle

noun _____

_____

verb _____

_____

light

noun _____

_____

adjective _____

_____

empty

verb _____

_____

adjective _____

_____

well

adverb _____

_____

noun _____

_____

Identify the subject; then parse the sentence and the verb.

The army's advance was causing a great disturbance.

singular | plural
1st person | 2nd person | 3rd person
past | present | future
simple | continuous

9

Sentence Walls

Parse these sentences. Then identify the verb, subject, and object (if there is one) for each one and write them on the wall. Add the words which describe, or "modify," them directly underneath.

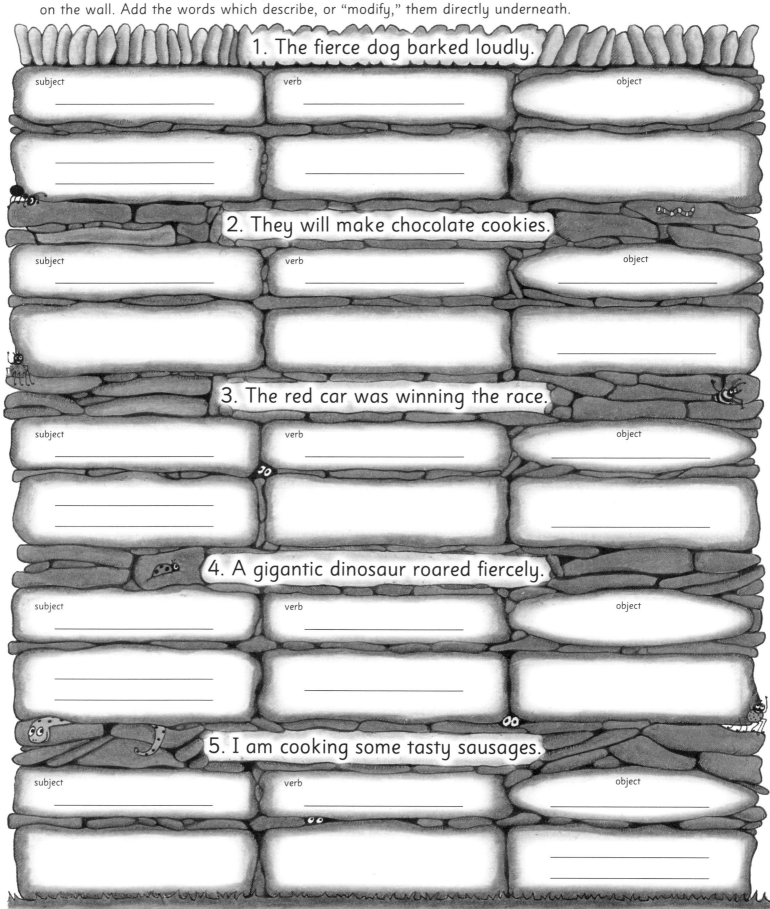

1. The fierce dog barked loudly.

subject _____ verb _____ object _____

_____ _____ _____

2. They will make chocolate cookies.

subject _____ verb _____ object _____

_____ _____ _____

3. The red car was winning the race.

subject _____ verb _____ object _____

_____ _____ _____

4. A gigantic dinosaur roared fiercely.

subject _____ verb _____ object _____

_____ _____ _____

5. I am cooking some tasty sausages.

subject _____ verb _____ object _____

_____ _____ _____

"Grow" the root words below by adding the suffixes to make a word family for each one.

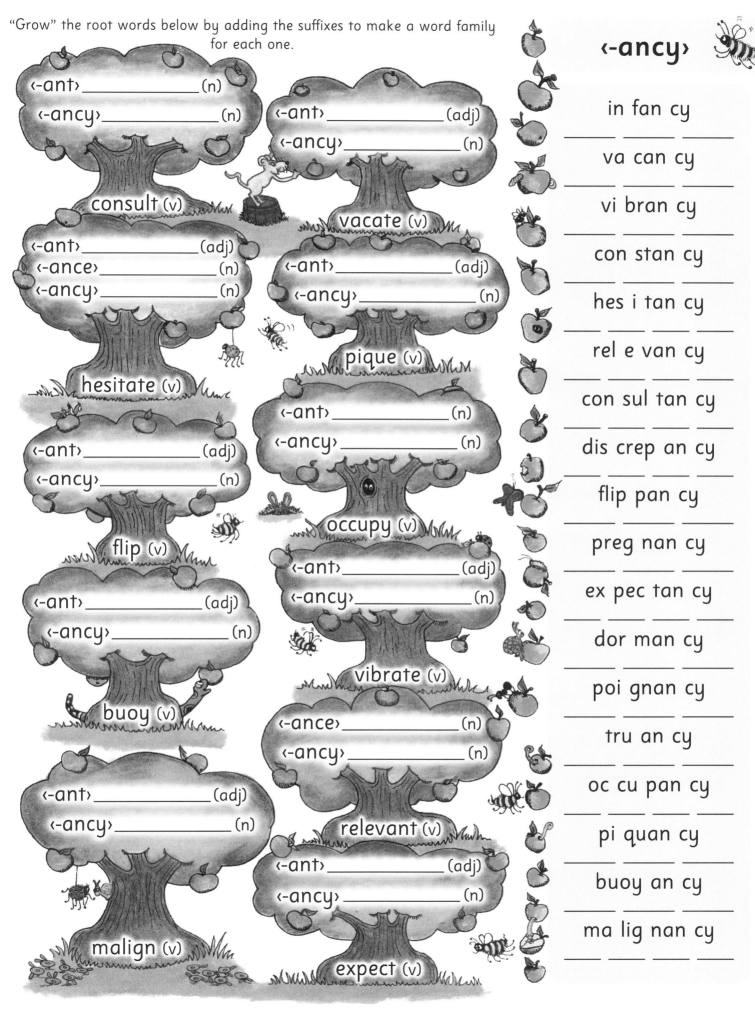

‹-ant› _____ (n)
‹-ancy› _____ (n)
consult (v)

‹-ant› _____ (adj)
‹-ance› _____ (n)
‹-ancy› _____ (n)
hesitate (v)

‹-ant› _____ (adj)
‹-ancy› _____ (n)
flip (v)

‹-ant› _____ (adj)
‹-ancy› _____ (n)
buoy (v)

‹-ant› _____ (adj)
‹-ancy› _____ (n)
malign (v)

‹-ant› _____ (adj)
‹-ancy› _____ (n)
vacate (v)

‹-ant› _____ (adj)
‹-ancy› _____ (n)
pique (v)

‹-ant› _____ (n)
‹-ancy› _____ (n)
occupy (v)

‹-ant› _____ (adj)
‹-ancy› _____ (n)
vibrate (v)

‹-ance› _____ (n)
‹-ancy› _____ (n)
relevant (v)

‹-ant› _____ (adj)
‹-ancy› _____ (n)
expect (v)

‹-ancy›

in fan cy
____ ____ ____
va can cy
____ ____ ____
vi bran cy
____ ____ ____
con stan cy
____ ____ ____
hes i tan cy
____ ____ ____ ____
rel e van cy
____ ____ ____ ____
con sul tan cy
____ ____ ____ ____
dis crep an cy
____ ____ ____ ____
flip pan cy
____ ____ ____
preg nan cy
____ ____ ____
ex pec tan cy
____ ____ ____ ____
dor man cy
____ ____ ____
poi gnan cy
____ ____ ____
tru an cy
____ ____ ____
oc cu pan cy
____ ____ ____ ____
pi quan cy
____ ____ ____
buoy an cy
____ ____ ____
ma lig nan cy
____ ____ ____ ____

11

Dictation: ‹-ancy›

1. _____

_____

2. _____

_____

3. _____

_____

1. The small birds chirped noisily.

subject	verb	object
_____	_____	
_____	_____	

2. The beautiful flowers have a lovely fragrance.

subject	verb	object
_____	_____	_____
_____	_____	_____

3. Our village bakery makes delicious apple pies.

subject	verb	object
_____	_____	_____
_____	_____	_____

Verb Tenses

Write each sentence in the correct tense tent. Then rewrite each sentence in the other tenses in the correct tense tents.

| You pat the dog. | They were trying hard. | I am enjoying my work. |
| She will be living abroad. | We felt cold. | He will walk home. |

Simple Past

Past Continuous

Simple Present

Present Continuous

Simple Future

Future Continuous

13

‹-ence›

ab sence
_____ _____

si lence
_____ _____

sen tence
_____ _____

ev i dence
_____ _____ _____

dif fer ence
_____ _____ _____

fence
_____

ex ist ence
_____ _____ _____

co her ence
_____ _____ _____

con fi dence
_____ _____ _____

el o quence
_____ _____ _____

pref er ence
_____ _____ _____

au di ence
_____ _____ _____

co in ci dence
_____ _____ _____ _____

e mer gence
_____ _____ _____

ex pe ri ence
_____ _____ _____ _____

op u lence
_____ _____ _____

in tel li gence
_____ _____ _____ _____

con ve ni ence
_____ _____ _____ _____

Match these words from the spelling list with their root words.

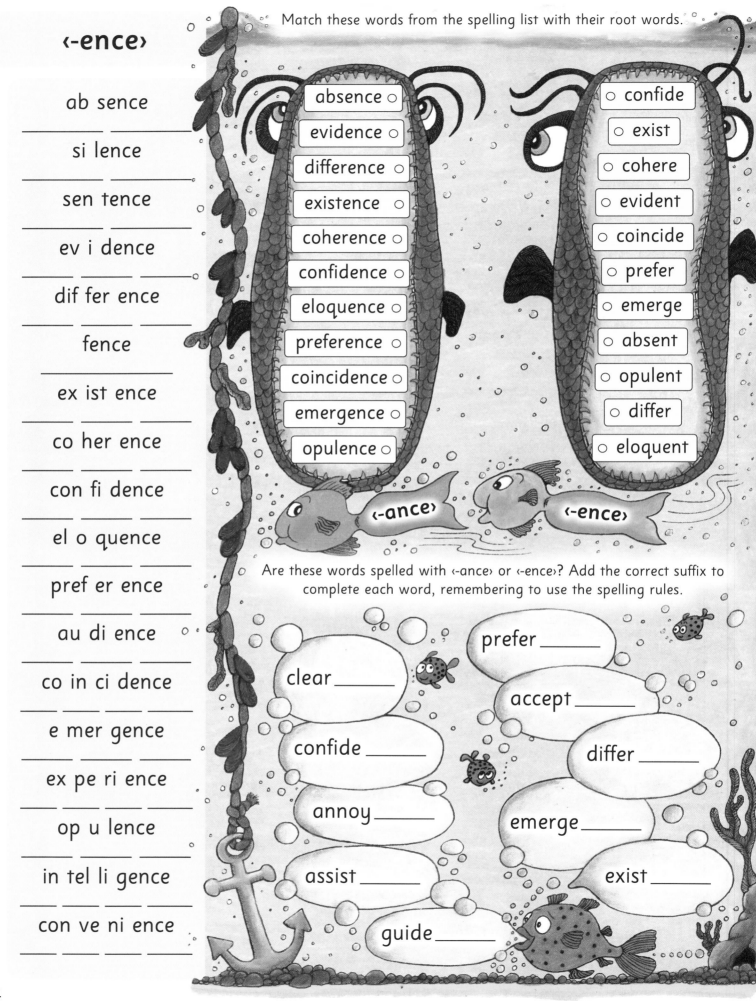

absence ○   ○ confide
evidence ○   ○ exist
difference ○   ○ cohere
existence ○   ○ evident
coherence ○   ○ coincide
confidence ○   ○ prefer
eloquence ○   ○ emerge
preference ○   ○ absent
coincidence ○   ○ opulent
emergence ○   ○ differ
opulence ○   ○ eloquent

‹-ance› ‹-ence›

Are these words spelled with ‹-ance› or ‹-ence›? Add the correct suffix to complete each word, remembering to use the spelling rules.

prefer_____
clear_____
accept_____
confide_____
differ_____
annoy_____
emerge_____
assist_____
exist_____
guide_____

14

Dictation: ‹-ence›

Are these words spelled with ‹-ance› or ‹-ence›? Add the correct suffix to complete each word, and remember to use the spelling rules.

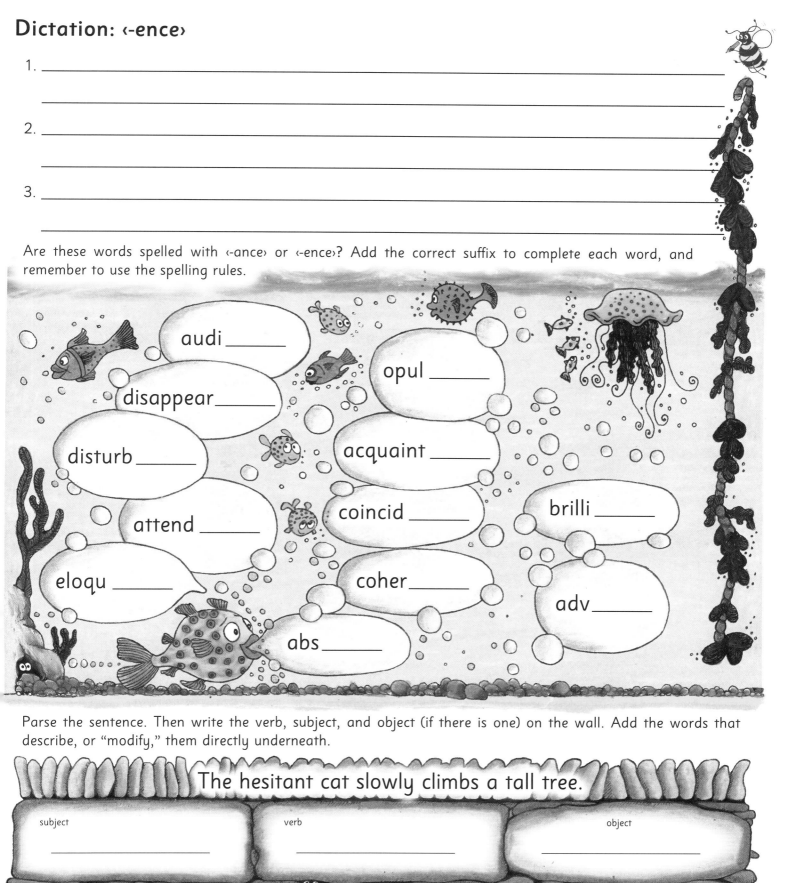

audi_____

opul_____

disappear_____

disturb_____

acquaint_____

attend_____

coincid_____

brilli_____

eloqu_____

coher_____

adv_____

abs_____

Parse the sentence. Then write the verb, subject, and object (if there is one) on the wall. Add the words that describe, or "modify," them directly underneath.

The hesitant cat slowly climbs a tall tree.

subject	verb	object
_____	_____	_____
_____	_____	_____

Verbs

"To Have"

Conjugate the verb "to have" in the simple past, present, and future.

I   you

simple past	simple present	simple future
I had	I have	I shall have

In each sentence, underline the verb "to have" in red. Then decide if the sentence is in the past, present, or future.

I have brown eyes.

She has blonde hair.

They had a brilliant idea.

He will have a party.

We had some good news today.

You will have a great time.

I had spaghetti for dinner.

It has bigger paws than a normal cat.

past present future

he / she / it

you

we

they

Now conjugate the verb "to have" in the continuous tenses.

	past continuous	present continuous	future continuous
I		am having	
you			
he/she/it			
we			
you			
they			

"Grow" the root words below by adding the suffixes to make a word family for each one.

‹-ent›_____(adj)
‹-ency›_____(n)

urge (v)

‹-ent›_____(adj)
‹-ence›_____(n)
‹-ency›_____(n)

emerge (v)

‹-ent›_____(n) (adj)
‹-ence›_____(n)
‹-ency›_____(n)

reside (v)

‹-ent›_____(adj)
‹-ency›_____(n)

frequent (v)

‹-ent›_____(adj)
‹-ency›_____(n)

consist (v)

‹-ent›_____(n) (adj)
‹-ence›_____(n)
‹-ency›_____(n)

depend (v)

‹-ent›_____(adj)
‹-ence›_____(n)
‹-ency›_____(n)

cohere (v)

‹-ence›_____(n)
‹-ency›_____(n)

competent (adj)

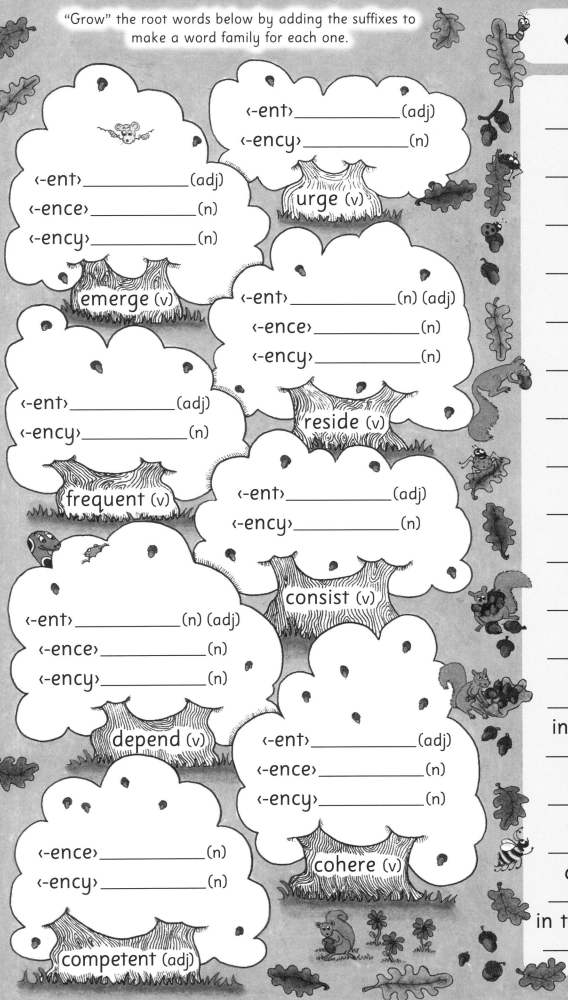

‹-ency›

a gen cy
___ ___ ___
cur ren cy
___ ___ ___
e mer gen cy
___ ___ ___ ___
po ten cy
___ ___ ___
ten den cy
___ ___ ___
ur gen cy
___ ___ ___
re gen cy
___ ___ ___
flu en cy
___ ___ ___
fre quen cy
___ ___ ___
pun gen cy
___ ___ ___
res i den cy
___ ___ ___ ___
ef fi cien cy
___ ___ ___ ___
co her en cy
___ ___ ___ ___
in com pe ten cy
___ ___ ___ ___ ___
pro fi cien cy
___ ___ ___ ___
con sis ten cy
___ ___ ___ ___
con tin gen cy
___ ___ ___ ___
in ter de pen den cy
___ ___ ___ ___ ___ ___

Dictation: ‹-ency›

1. _____

_____

2. _____

_____

3. _____

_____

Conjugate the verb "to have" in the simple and continuous tenses.

	Past	**Present**	**Future**
I	had	have	shall have
you	_____	_____	_____
he / she / it	_____	_____	_____
we	_____	_____	_____
you	_____	_____	_____
they	_____	_____	_____
I	was having	am having	shall be having
you	_____	_____	_____
he / she / it	_____	_____	_____
we	_____	_____	_____
you	_____	_____	_____
they	_____	_____	_____

Parse the sentence. Then write the verb, subject, and object (if there is one) on the wall. Add the words that describe, or "modify," them directly underneath.

He sang the old song beautifully.

subject	verb	object
_____	_____	_____
	_____	_____

Present and Past Participles

Make the present and past participles for each of these verbs by adding the suffixes ‹-ing› and ‹-ed›, using the spelling rules.

Verb	Present Participle + ‹-ing›	Past Participle + ‹-ed›
to accept		
to enter		
to die		
to marry		
to annoy		
to damage		
to disturb		
to copy		
to chop		
to permit		
to compete		
to applaud		
to spray		
to exercise		
to terrify		
to worry		
to unwrap		
to disapprove		

Butterfly House

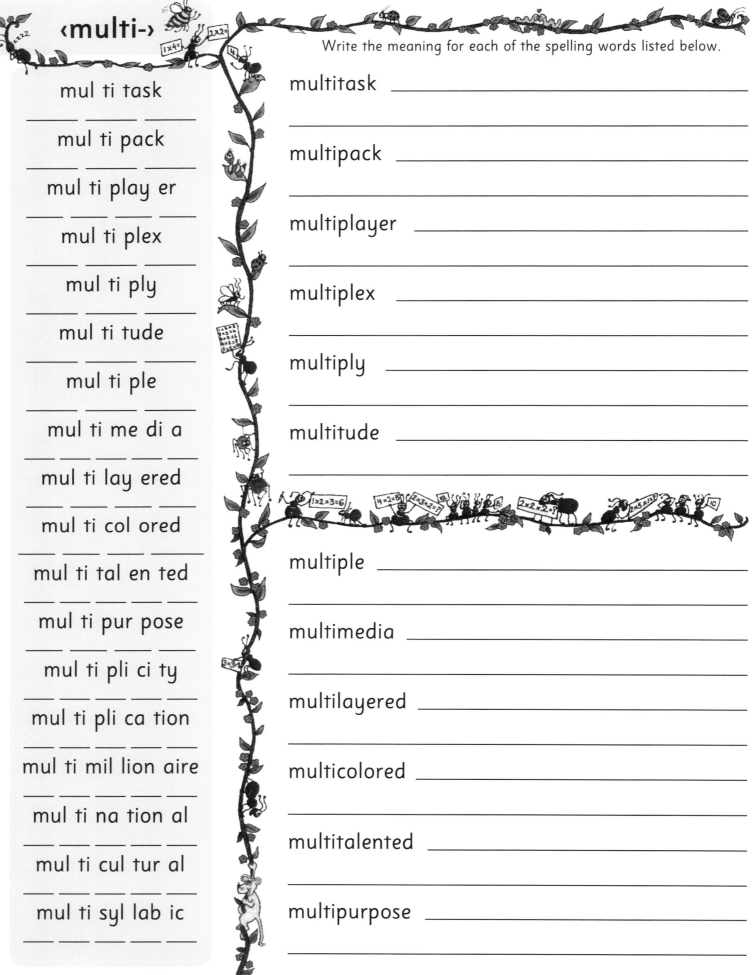

‹multi-›

mul ti task

____ ____ ____

mul ti pack

____ ____ ____

mul ti play er

____ ____ ____ ____

mul ti plex

____ ____ ____

mul ti ply

____ ____ ____

mul ti tude

____ ____ ____

mul ti ple

____ ____ ____

mul ti me di a

____ ____ ____ ____ ____

mul ti lay ered

____ ____ ____ ____

mul ti col ored

____ ____ ____ ____

mul ti tal en ted

____ ____ ____ ____

mul ti pur pose

____ ____ ____

mul ti pli ci ty

____ ____ ____ ____

mul ti pli ca tion

____ ____ ____ ____

mul ti mil lion aire

____ ____ ____ ____ ____

mul ti na tion al

____ ____ ____ ____

mul ti cul tur al

____ ____ ____ ____

mul ti syl lab ic

____ ____ ____ ____

Write the meaning for each of the spelling words listed below.

multitask _____

_____

multipack _____

_____

multiplayer _____

_____

multiplex _____

_____

multiply _____

_____

multitude _____

_____

multiple _____

_____

multimedia _____

_____

multilayered _____

_____

multicolored _____

_____

multitalented _____

_____

multipurpose _____

_____

Dictation: ‹multi-›

1. _____

_____

2. _____

_____

3. _____

_____

Use a dictionary to find out what this word means and see how many other words you can make with its letters.

m u l t i m i l l i o n a i r e

I will visit the big new multiplex.

subject	verb	object
_____	_____	_____
		_____

Perfect Tenses

Write the verb "to finish" in the past, present, and future perfect. Then write a sentence at the bottom of each tense tent that uses the verb in the appropriate tense.

Past Perfect

I had finished
you
he
she
it
we
you
they

Present Perfect

I have finished
you
he
she
it
we
you
they

Future Perfect

I shall have finished
you
he
she
it
we
you
they

Match the words in the spelling list to the descriptions below.

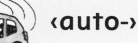

‹auto-›

another name for a robot
_____

done as a habit, without thinking
_____

a machine that can fly a plane by itself
_____

done by machine or computer, instead of people
_____

the freedom to make your own decisions
_____

a short way of saying "automobile" or "automotive"
_____

an old-fashioned word for a car
_____

of, or relating to, cars
_____

a medical examination of a dead body
_____

a famous person's signature
_____

the ruler of a country, who has complete power
_____

the use of machines rather than people to do a job
_____

without thinking, as a habit
_____

a book written by someone about his or her life
_____

a word for "independent" or "having autonomy"
_____

a country where the ruler has complete power
_____

the part of a camera that focuses automatically
_____

relating to illness caused by a body's own defences
_____

au to
_____

au to mat ic
___ ___ ___ ___

au ton o my
___ ___ ___ ___

au to mat ed
___ ___ ___ ___

au tom a ton
___ ___ ___ ___

au to pi lot
___ ___ ___ ___

au to ma tion
___ ___ ___ ___

au to mo bile
___ ___ ___ ___

au to graph
___ ___ ___

au to mo tive
___ ___ ___ ___

au top sy
___ ___ ___

au to crat
___ ___ ___

au to im mune
___ ___ ___ ___

au to fo cus
___ ___ ___ ___

au toc ra cy
___ ___ ___ ___

au ton o mous
___ ___ ___ ___

au to mat i cal ly
___ ___ ___ ___ ___ ___

au to bi og ra phy
___ ___ ___ ___ ___ ___

Dictation: ‹auto-›

1. _____

_____

2. _____

_____

3. _____

_____

Imagine you are writing a book about your life so far. What would you want to put in it? Make a list of some things you could talk about. Then draw a picture of yourself in the mirror.

In my autobiography, I would talk about these things:

_____

_____

_____

_____

_____

_____

_____

_____

_____

This is my autograph:

_____

This is me!

The experienced captain has used the plane's autopilot.

subject	verb	object
_____	_____	_____
_____	_____	_____

Contractions and the Verb "To Have"

I have

I've

Trace over the contractions in the flowers. Then, in the flower pot, write the whole words as contractions and write the contractions out in full, with no letters missing.

REMEMBER!
She's, he's, and it's could stand for "she has," "he has," and "it has" OR "she is," "he is," and "it is."

I'd   you'd   she'd   we'd   they'd   it'll have

I've   you've   he's   we've   they've

I had _____   you have _____   they had _____
we have _____   he has _____   I shall have_____
you'd _____   it'll have _____   we'd_____
they've _____   she'd _____   I've _____

Rewrite these sentences, either expanding or contracting the verb "to have."

"We've prepared a lovely picnic for lunch," said Meg.

_____
_____

They had visited the museum several times before.

_____
_____

Dad grumbled, "I don't think you'll have finished by then."

_____
_____

Tina was tired because she had jogged all the way to the park.

_____
_____

"It's stopped raining now," called Ben.

_____
_____

By the end of today, I shall have painted the fence.

_____
_____

25

Put these words from the spelling list into the prefix fish.
Write the prefix in the head and the root word in the body.

meg a star
_____ _____ _____

meg a bit
_____ _____ _____

meg a bucks
_____ _____ _____

mi cro chip
_____ _____ _____

mi cro film
_____ _____ _____

meg a lith
_____ _____ _____

mi cro scope
_____ _____ _____

mi crobe
_____ _____

mi cro wave
_____ _____ _____

mi cro phone
_____ _____ _____

meg a phone
_____ _____ _____

meg a watt
_____ _____ _____

mi cro scop ic
_____ _____ _____ _____

mi cro bi ol o gy
_____ _____ _____ _____ _____ _____

mi cro pro ces sor
_____ _____ _____ _____ _____

meg a byte
_____ _____ _____

meg a hertz
_____ _____ _____

meg a lo ma ni a
_____ _____ _____ _____ _____ _____

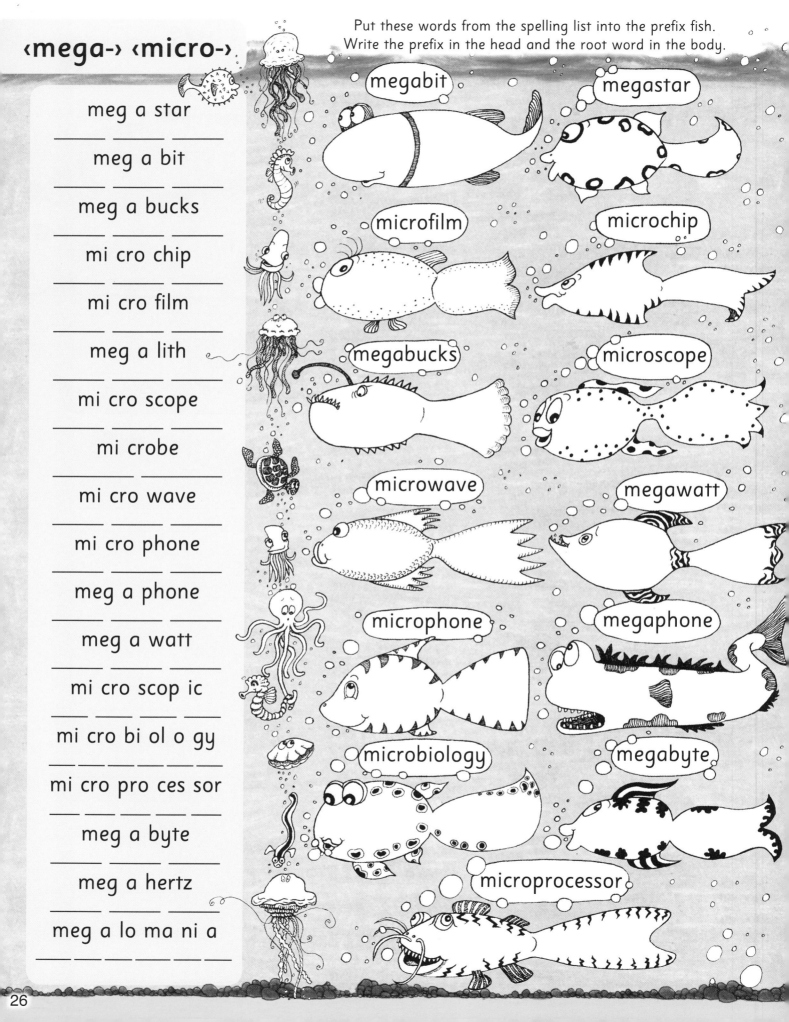

megabit

megastar

microfilm

microchip

megabucks

microscope

microwave

megawatt

microphone

megaphone

microbiology

megabyte

microprocessor

Dictation: ‹mega-› ‹micro-›

1. _____

   _____

2. _____

   _____

3. _____

   _____

Rewrite these sentences in the past, present, or future perfect.

Perfect Tenses

past	present	future
I had walked	I have walked	I shall have walked

Zack plays on his computer.

past perfect _____

present perfect _____

future perfect _____

The children copy the dance steps.

past perfect _____

present perfect _____

future perfect _____

The college student previously studied microbiology.

subject	verb	object
_____	_____	_____
_____	_____	_____

Irregular Past Participles

Not all verbs make their past tenses and past participles by adding
‹-ed›. These verbs are irregular, or "tricky," and have to be learned.
Often they change the vowel sound and sometimes they have other letters too.

These
verbs have ‹i› in the root word,
‹a› in the simple past, and ‹u› in the past participle.

infinitive/present	simple past	past participle
swim		
ring		
sink		
begin	began	
drink	drank	
sing	sang	
stink		stunk
spring		sprung
shrink		shrunk

These verbs
change the vowel sound in the simple past
and add ‹-n› or ‹-en› to the infinitive for the past participle.

infinitive/present	simple past	past participle
grow	grew	grown
bite		
draw		
write		
fall		
know		
take		
give		
shake		
hide		

Unscramble the letters in the stars and add them to ‹super› to make words from the spelling list.

‹super-›

su per
_____
su perb
_____
su per star
__ __ ___ __
su per son ic
__ __ __ __
su per glue
__ __ __
su per mod el
__ __ __ __
su pe ri or
__ __ __ __
su per sede
__ __ __
su per im pose
__ __ __ __
su per pow er
__ __ __ __
su per vise
__ __ __
su per la tive
__ __ __ __
su pe ri or i ty
__ __ __ __ __ __
su per struc ture
__ __ __ __
su per vi sion
__ __ __ __
su per cil i ous
__ __ __ __ __
su per mar ket
__ __ __ __
su per flu ous
__ __ __ __

Stars (scrambled letters):

m l e o d → super_____
b → super_____
i c o s n → super_____
s a r t → super_____
l e u g → super_____
i r o → super_____
p s e i m o → super_____
i e s v → super_____
s e e d → super_____
a l e i v t → super_____
p r w o e → super_____

29

Dictation: ‹super-›

1. _____

_____

2. _____

_____

3. _____

_____

Write each verb in both forms.

These tricky verbs change the vowel sound in the simple past and then add ‹-n› or ‹-en› to it for the past participle.

infinitive / present	simple past	past participle
tear		
wake		
break		
forget		
wear		
freeze		
steal		
choose		
speak		
swear		

The strict granny was supervising her lively grandchildren.

subject	verb	object
_____	_____	_____
_____	_____	_____

30

Identifying Verb Tenses

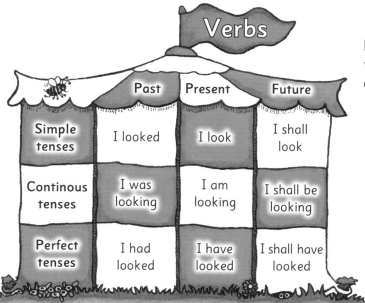

	Past	Present	Future
Simple tenses	I looked	I look	I shall look
Continous tenses	I was looking	I am looking	I shall be looking
Perfect tenses	I had looked	I have looked	I shall have looked

Find the verbs in these sentences and underline them in red. Then decide which tenses they are in and write them in the tense tents.

I <u>am balancing</u> on a ball like an acrobat.

The rats were scavenging for food.

A truck has damaged the fence post.

He will be going to college next year.

We change our minds all the time.

You will have written the story by then.

Her confidence had grown over the years.

A butterfly will emerge from the chrysalis.

She received a strange message yesterday.

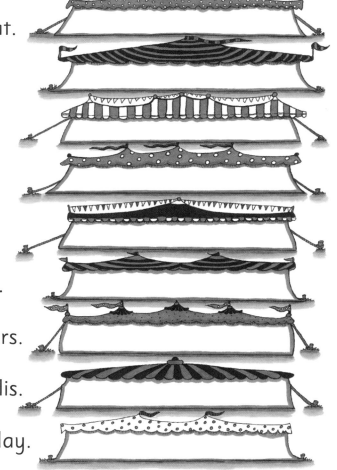

Past	**Present**	**Future**
Action: Point your thumb backward over your shoulder.	Action: Point toward the floor with the palm of your hand.	Action: Point to the front with your finger.

‹cent-› ‹kilo-› ‹milli-›

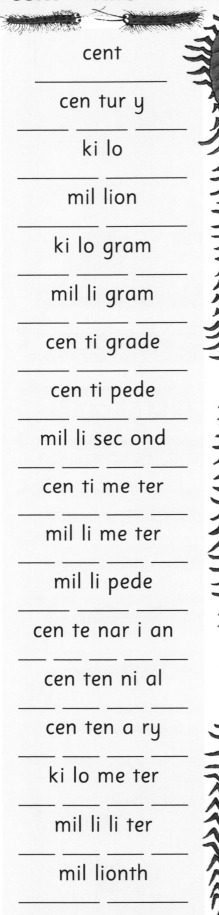

cent
_____

cen tur y
___ ___ ___

ki lo
___ ___

mil lion
___ ___

ki lo gram
___ ___ ___

mil li gram
___ ___ ___

cen ti grade
___ ___ ___

cen ti pede
___ ___ ___

mil li sec ond
___ ___ ___ ___

cen ti me ter
___ ___ ___ ___

mil li me ter
___ ___ ___ ___

mil li pede
___ ___ ___

cen te nar i an
___ ___ ___ ___ ___

cen ten ni al
___ ___ ___ ___

cen ten a ry
___ ___ ___ ___

ki lo me ter
___ ___ ___ ___

mil li li ter
___ ___ ___ ___

mil lionth
___ ___

Write a sentence for each of the spelling words below.

cent _____

_____

century _____

_____

kilo _____

_____

million _____

_____

kilogram _____

_____

milligram _____

_____

centigrade _____

_____

centipede _____

_____

millisecond _____

_____

centimeter _____

_____

millimeter _____

_____

millipede _____

_____

Dictation: ‹cent-› ‹kilo-› ‹milli-›

1. _____

_____

2. _____

_____

3. _____

_____

? 100 ? 1,000 ? 1,000,000 ?

Think about what the prefixes ‹cent-›, ‹kilo-›, and ‹milli-› mean to help you answer these questions.

How many years are in a century?   _____

How many grams are in a kilogram?   _____

How old is a centenarian?   _____

How many millimeters are in a meter?   _____

How many legs might a centipede have?   _____

How many thousands are in a million?   _____

How many meters are in a kilometer?   _____

Numbers can be written as words, like "three," or numerals, like "3." Rewrite the numbers below as numerals. Then draw a centipede on the grass.

one hundred _____   one thousand _____   one million _____

Her naughty daughter had broken the tenth-century Chinese vase.

subject	verb	object
_____	_____	_____
_____	_____	_____

33

Adverbs

Where are the Adverbs?

Words that tell us more about **how**, **where**, **when**, **how often**, or **how much** something happens are called adverbs. Although these adverbs describe the verb, they do not always go next to it. Can you find the verbs and adverbs in these sentences?

A girl <u>was humming</u> the tune <u>quietly</u>.

They enjoyed the flowers' fragrance enormously.

The weather has gradually improved during the day.

The knight had courageously fought the fierce dragon.

Grudgingly, he offered his assistance to the old man.

She is finally meeting her pen pal from Australia.

The audience were loudly applauding the band.

The adverb "not" is used to make a word, statement, or question negative, so it has the opposite meaning. Make these sentences negative by adding "not" in the correct place.

The supermodel has written her autobiography.

_____

_____

He is improving his fluency in the language.

_____

_____

We had noticed a discrepancy in the numbers.

_____

_____

I am working at the agency around the corner.

_____

_____

Put these words from the spelling list into the prefix fish.
Write the prefix in the head and the root in the body.

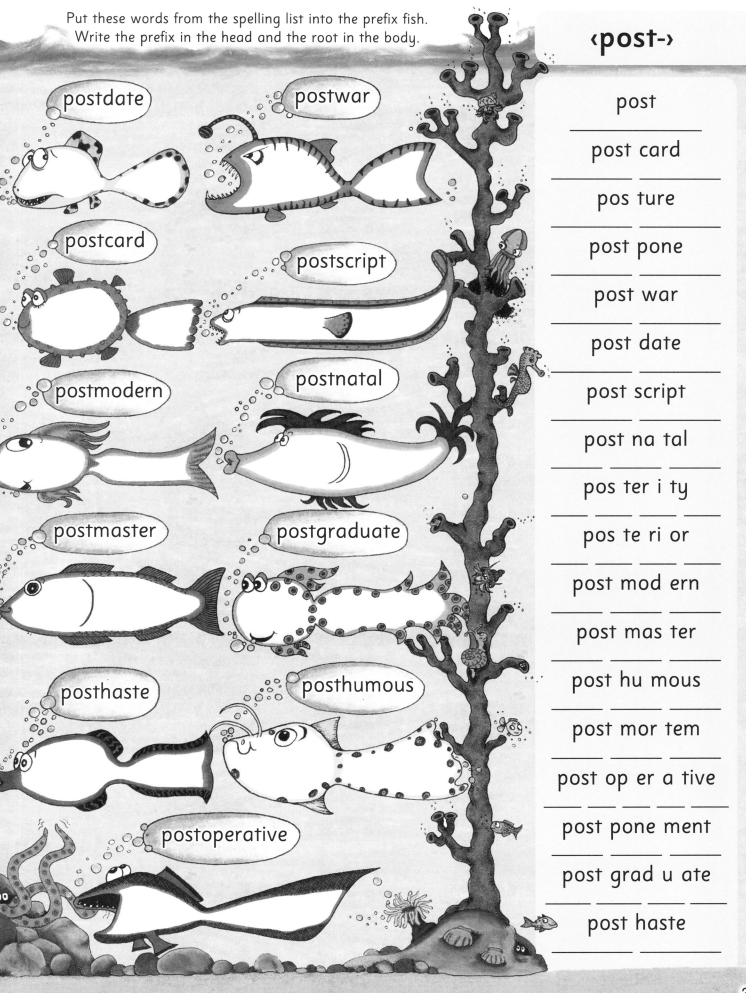

‹post-›

post
post card
pos ture
post pone
post war
post date
post script
post na tal
pos ter i ty
pos te ri or
post mod ern
post mas ter
post hu mous
post mor tem
post op er a tive
post pone ment
post grad u ate
post haste

35

Dictation: ‹post-›

Choose one of the prefixes to complete each word.

ir-   in-   mid-   semi-

im-   il-   dis-   un-

_____responsible

_____fair   _____way   _____lock

_____active   _____appear   _____night

                     _____logical   _____probable

                     _____correct   _____circle

The tennis club is not postponing tomorrow's match.

subject	verb	object
_____	_____	_____
_____	_____	_____

36

Proofreading

It is always important to proofread your writing, checking that it makes sense and has no mistakes. Look at these sentences, make sure all the words agree, and identify any errors in spelling and punctuation. Then write them out correctly on the lines below.

They was singing in the school consert

_____
_____

He drived the car very quikly around the corner.

_____
_____

the microfone was working not properly.

_____
_____

She is runing down the street wen she tripped over.

_____
_____

the snail disappeard into it's shell.

_____
_____

I had ate a egg sanwich.

_____
_____

The boy's a new pensil case.

_____
_____

where are the appels from the supermarcket

_____
_____

We postponned the race due to the bad whether.

_____
_____

‹-tion›

option
_____

position
_____

action
_____

section
_____

mention
_____

question
_____

direction
_____

suggestion
_____

infection
_____

rejection
_____

condition
_____

function
_____

competition
_____

contribution
_____

introduction
_____

opposition
_____

production
_____

connection
_____

Which nouns in the spelling list come from these root verbs?

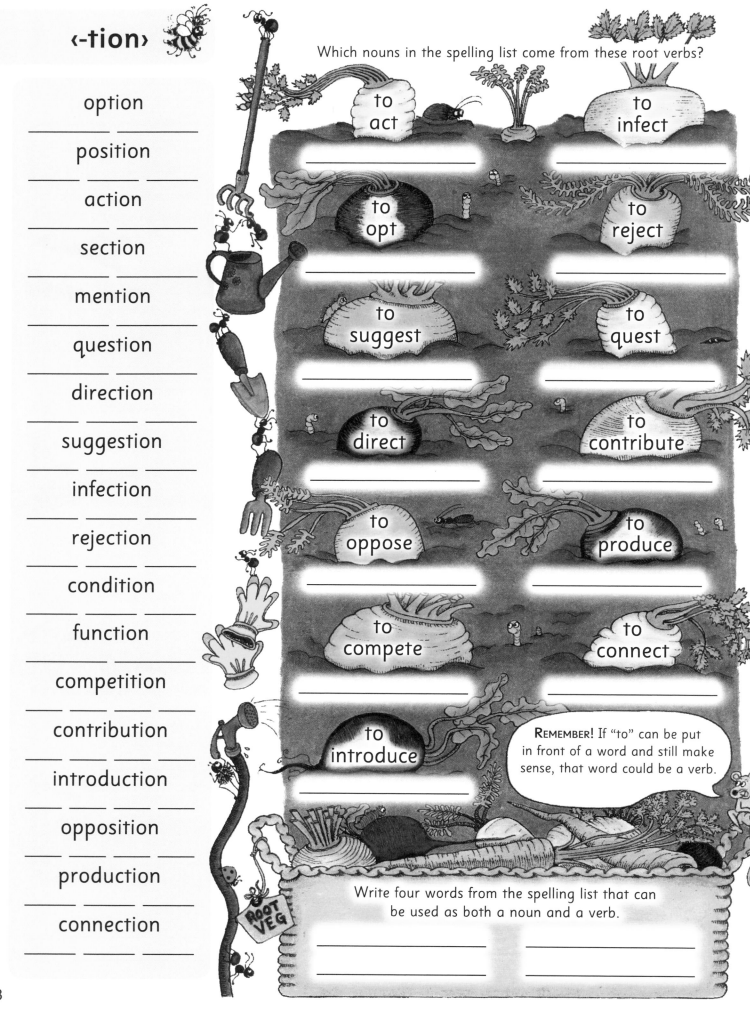

to act
_____

to infect
_____

to opt
_____

to reject
_____

to suggest
_____

to quest
_____

to direct
_____

to contribute
_____

to oppose
_____

to produce
_____

to compete
_____

to connect
_____

to introduce
_____

REMEMBER! If "to" can be put in front of a word and still make sense, that word could be a verb.

Write four words from the spelling list that can be used as both a noun and a verb.

_____   _____

_____   _____

ROOT VEG

38

Dictation: ‹-tion›

1. _____

_____

2. _____

_____

3. _____

_____

Rewrite these contractions of the verb "to have" in full.

I've _____   it's _____   you'd _____

they'd _____   she'd _____   I'd _____

he'll have _____ you've _____   we've _____

Rewrite these parts of the verb "to have" as contractions.

she has _____   they have _____   you had _____

it had _____   we had _____   he will have _____

we have _____   I shall have _____   he had _____

The store detective has questioned the customer thoroughly.

subject	verb	object

Prepositions

Can you find the prepositions in this word search? The words go across and down the grid. Put a line through each word on the list as you find it.

s	b	y	k	l	n	p	a	s	q	i	n	s	i	d	e	c
l	q	x	a	b	o	u	t	z	b	m	e	k	w	o	f	s
t	c	g	b	h	p	b	e	l	o	w	a	d	x	w	f	u
h	f	r	o	m	z	k	j	r	w	a	r	o	u	n	d	n
r	o	x	v	m	p	o	u	t	s	i	d	e	t	j	k	d
o	l	y	e	f	l	q	p	a	s	t	b	u	r	f	l	e
u	l	a	c	r	o	s	s	x	a	g	a	i	n	s	t	r
g	o	p	p	o	s	i	t	e	g	b	w	c	p	l	h	n
h	w	z	b	n	j	b	o	v	e	r	d	x	q	j	r	e
o	i	n	e	y	k	w	i	t	h	y	t	o	n	t	o	a
u	n	b	t	z	b	e	n	e	a	t	h	j	t	q	u	t
t	g	c	w	b	e	f	o	r	e	k	a	l	o	n	g	h
i	b	j	e	s	h	r	k	b	o	f	f	x	w	g	h	u
g	l	m	e	k	i	n	t	o	s	f	t	c	a	p	m	l
e	y	d	n	u	n	t	i	l	z	k	e	f	r	j	r	x
s	f	j	u	n	d	e	r	p	f	o	r	f	d	x	y	j
s	q	u	d	u	r	i	n	g	a	m	b	e	s	i	d	e

behind	toward	inside	about	through	outside
up	over	by	to	off	for
below	across	onto	after	under	along
into	of	at	in	as	on
around	beside	above	before	during	against
past	with	until	down	near	from
following	between	opposite	underneath	beneath	throughout

Write the meaning for each of the spelling words listed below.

version _____

_____

mansion _____

_____

tension _____

_____

pension _____

_____

aversion _____

_____

pretension _____

_____

occasion _____

_____

compulsion _____

_____

conversion _____

_____

diversion _____

_____

propulsion _____

_____

extension _____

_____

‹-sion›

version
_____ _____

mansion
_____ _____

tension
_____ _____

pension
_____ _____

aversion
_____ _____

pretension
_____ _____

occasion
_____ _____

compulsion
_____ _____

conversion
_____ _____

diversion
_____ _____

propulsion
_____ _____

extension
_____ _____

dimension
_____ _____

collision
_____ _____

expansion
_____ _____

apprehension
_____ _____ _____

comprehension
_____ _____ _____

misapprehension
_____ _____ _____ _____

Dictation: ‹-sion›

1. _____
   _____

2. _____
   _____

3. _____
   _____

Underline each verb in red and decide if the sentences are in the simple past, present, or future. Then rewrite them in the past, present, or future perfect.

The two friends walked down the path.
_____

We water the plants every day.
_____

She will wait for her sister before leaving.
_____

The deer disappeared between the trees.
_____

I will finish at about four o'clock.
_____

The rich landowner had recently built a huge mansion.

subject	verb	object

42

Prepositional Phrases

A prepositional phrase starts with a preposition and is usually followed by a noun phrase or pronoun. Complete these sentences by adding a different prepositional phrase to each one.

Our library is open _____.

Two strangers stood _____.

She bought the tickets _____.

I will meet you _____.

The young robin flew _____.

My brothers are going _____.

Their ball has bounced _____.

He left something _____.

We saw something _____.

A black cat had jumped _____.

Find the preposition in each sentence and underline it in green. Then identify all the words in the prepositional phrase and put a green box around them.

A little dog ran across the park.

The traffic was at a standstill.

She had received a letter from her sister.

Are you going to Carla's party?

He has locked the door with his key.

You must arrive by two o'clock.

Will his present arrive in time?

It is the first house on the right.

Those burglars are under arrest.

I am having a surprise for my birthday.

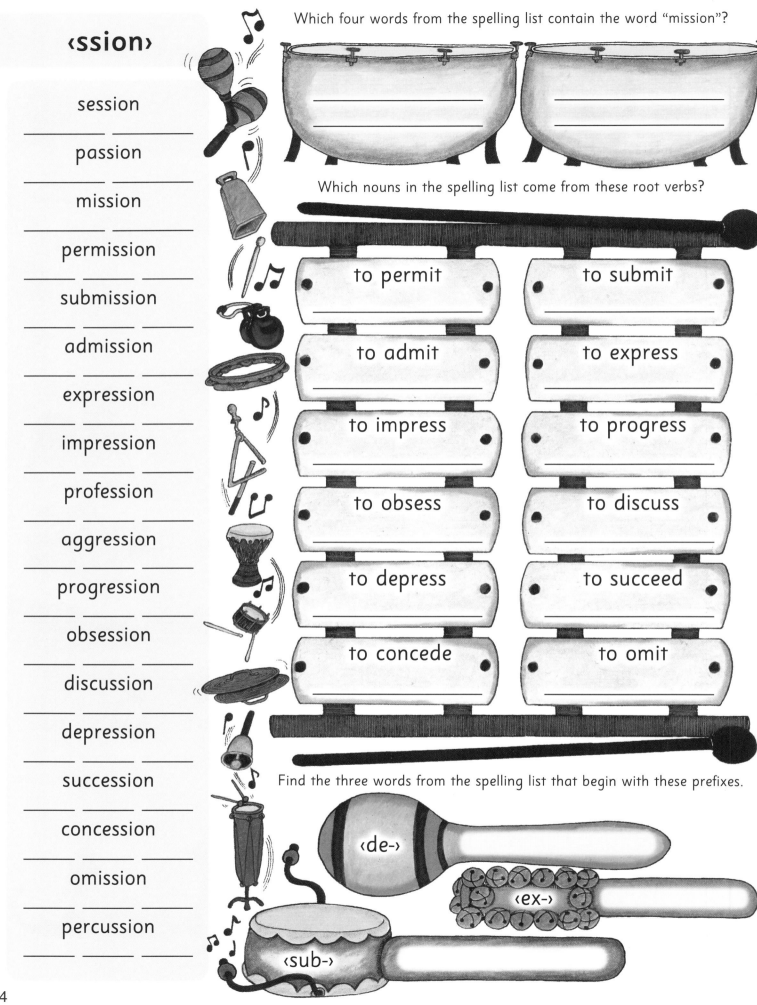

‹ssion›

session

passion

mission

permission

submission

admission

expression

impression

profession

aggression

progression

obsession

discussion

depression

succession

concession

omission

percussion

Which four words from the spelling list contain the word "mission"?

Which nouns in the spelling list come from these root verbs?

to permit

to submit

to admit

to express

to impress

to progress

to obsess

to discuss

to depress

to succeed

to concede

to omit

Find the three words from the spelling list that begin with these prefixes.

‹de-›

‹ex-›

‹sub-›

44

Dictation: ‹ssion›

1. _____

_____

2. _____

_____

3. _____

_____

Underline each preposition in green and add a noun phrase to it to make a prepositional phrase.

at _____   in _____

on _____   to _____

past _____   under _____

along _____   around _____

before _____   across _____

through _____   during _____

Now use one of the prepositional phrases in a sentence.

_____

_____

The percussion player was wearing a determined expression.

subject	verb	object

Noun Phrases as Subjects and Objects

Parse each sentence and identify the noun phrase acting as either the subject or object. Write the sentence on the wall, remembering to put only the head noun in the subject/object box. This is called the **simple subject** or **object**. Add the rest of the noun phrase underneath.

1. Two savage lions roared loudly.

subject	verb	object

Noun phrase _____

Simple subject _____

2. We recently visited a new French restaurant.

subject	verb	object

Noun phrase _____

Simple object _____

3. The multitalented megastar has mysteriously disappeared.

subject	verb	object

Noun phrase _____

Simple subject _____

Write the meaning for each of the spelling words listed below.

‹cian›

musician _____

_____

magician _____

_____

dietician _____

_____

optician _____

_____

tactician _____

_____

technician _____

_____

clinician _____

_____

mortician _____

_____

patrician _____

_____

politician _____

_____

physician _____

_____

electrician _____

_____

musician
__ __

magician
__ __

dietician
__ __

optician
__ __

tactician
__ __

technician
__ __

clinician
__ __

mortician
__ __

patrician
__ __

politician
__ __

physician
__ __

electrician
__ __

beautician
__ __

statistician
__ __

arithmetician
__ __

mathematician
__ __

obstetrician
__ __

pediatrician
__ __

47

Dictation: ‹cian›

1. _____

_____

2. _____

_____

3. _____

_____

Think of an antonym (opposite meaning) and synonym (same or similar meaning)
for each word.

antonym

synonym

change   _____   _____

silence   _____   _____

courage   _____   _____

damage   _____   _____

multiple   _____   _____

superior   _____   _____

Tom has definitely made an excellent impression.

subject	verb	object

Compound Subjects and Objects

A sentence can have more than one subject and object. Parse each sentence and write it on the wall, remembering to put all the subjects and any objects in the relevant boxes.

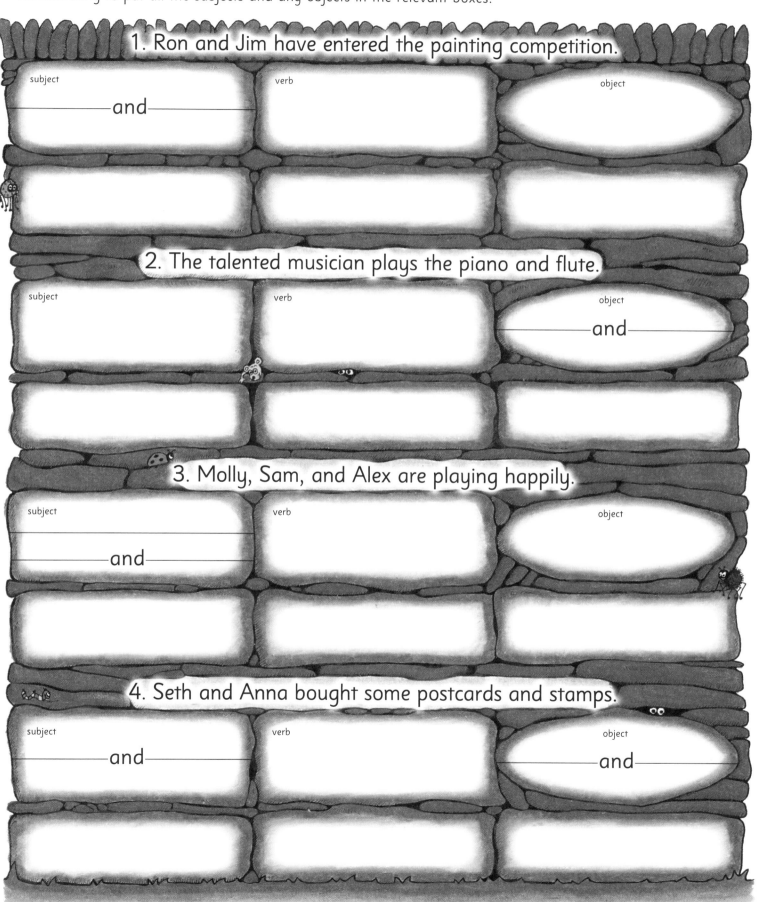

1. Ron and Jim have entered the painting competition.

subject ——and—— verb object

2. The talented musician plays the piano and flute.

subject verb object ——and——

3. Molly, Sam, and Alex are playing happily.

subject ——and—— verb object

4. Seth and Anna bought some postcards and stamps.

subject ——and—— verb object ——and——

‹-ation›

nation

_____

creation

_____

operation

_____

education

_____

relation

_____

location

_____

exploration

_____

explanation

_____

conversation

_____

information

_____

quotation

_____

association

_____

celebration

_____

investigation

_____

cancellation

_____

identification

_____

pronunciation

_____

observation

_____

What is the root verb for each of these nouns from the spelling list?

creation

to _____

operation

to _____

conversation

to _____

association

to _____

exploration

to _____

identification

to _____

investigation

to _____

cancellation

to _____

education

to _____

location

to _____

relation

to _____

quotation

to _____

explanation

to _____

information

to _____

observation

to _____

celebration

to _____

pronunciation

to _____

Dictation: ‹-ation›

1. _____

_____

2. _____

_____

3. _____

_____

In each sentence, underline the noun in black and put a black box around the noun phrase acting as the subject or object. Then write the noun phrase and simple subject/object.

They always had the most interesting conversations.

Noun phrase _____

Simple object _____

The lost Arctic explorer eventually returned safely.

Noun phrase _____

Simple subject _____

Her husband's closest relations will be arriving soon.

Noun phrase _____

Simple subject _____

The magical, mysterious magician totally amazed us.

Noun phrase _____

Simple subject _____

I did not understand his long, complicated explanation.

Noun phrase _____

Simple object _____

Emma and Sally make some interesting observations.

subject	verb	object
_____ and _____		

51

Verbs

Transitive and Intransitive Verbs

| verb + object = **transitive** verb |
| verb + no object = **intransitive** verb |

In each sentence, underline the verb in red and identify the subject and the object, if there is one. Then decide whether the verb is transitive or intransitive.

I have arranged the flowers carefully.

transitive
intransitive

transitive
intransitive

Suddenly, the magician vanished.

transitive
intransitive

The tiny baby is sleeping.

transitive
intransitive

Soon the autumn leaves will fall.

transitive
intransitive

He rode his bike in the opposite direction.

transitive
intransitive

This orchestra has some superb musicians.

transitive
intransitive

A multimillionaire bought the big mansion.

transitive
intransitive

Some horses in the field were galloping.

transitive
intransitive

The little brown egg had cracked.

transitive
intransitive

She cracked the eggs into a bowl.

transitive
intransitive

Jennifer won the poetry competition.

transitive
intransitive

The politician answered the questions fully.

transitive
intransitive

An electrician sneezed loudly in the dusty attic.

transitive
intransitive

The superstar signed her autograph for her fans.

transitive
intransitive

Match the words in the spelling list to the descriptions below.

a small wooden house, often in the mountains
_____

the chief cook working in a hotel or restaurant
_____

a long slide for moving things to a lower level
_____

a piece of equipment with moving parts
_____

a V-shaped line or stripe
_____

a soft, see-through fabric in silk or nylon
_____

a small magazine that advertises something
_____

a castle or large country house in France
_____

the hair that a man grows on his upper lip
_____

it helps someone jump safely from a plane
_____

someone employed to drive a car for someone else
_____

a big hanging light with lots of glass decoration
_____

the way all medieval knights tried to behave
_____

Look up these spelling words in the dictionary and read their meanings.
Then give each pastry chef a mustache, each in a different style.

‹ch› ‹che›

chef
_____

chute
_____

chalet
_____

chevron
_____

chiffon
_____

machine
_____

parachute
_____

mustache
_____

chateau
_____

brochure
_____

crochet
_____

cache
_____

chivalry
_____

chenille
_____

chauffeur
_____

cliche
_____

chandelier
_____

chaperone
_____

chenille
chaperone
cache
cliche
crochet

53

Dictation: ‹ch› ‹che›

1. _____

_____

2. _____

_____

3. _____

_____

In each sentence, underline the verb in red and identify the subject and the object, if there is one. Then decide whether the verb is transitive or intransitive.

The |chef| has chopped the |vegetables| finely. ᶻᶻᶻᶻ
> transitive
> intransitive

The chauffeur was driving very carefully.
> transitive
> intransitive

His parachute had opened just in time.
> transitive
> intransitive

The new pool will have several water chutes.
> transitive
> intransitive

The machine is working properly now.
> transitive
> intransitive

The knight's chivalry impressed the queen.
> transitive
> intransitive

The pirates found the secret cache of gold.
> transitive
> intransitive

The crystal chandelier hung in the great hall.
> transitive
> intransitive

The French chateau will not be hiring a new chauffeur and chef.

subject	verb	object
		—and—
	transitive / intransitive	

54

Prepositional Phrases as Adverbs

Identify the prepositional phrases acting as adverbs. Underline the prepositions in green and put round brackets around each phrase in orange. Then decide whether the prepositional phrase tells us more about **how**, **where**, or **when** the verb is happening.

Jack and Jill went (up the hill).   How? Where? When?

Bats and owls hunt during the night.   How? Where? When?

I have sent the letter by airmail.   How? Where? When?

My friends have gone without me.   How? Where? When?

We visited the French chateau until 3pm.   How? Where? When?

A cat was creeping along the fence.   How? Where? When?

The family were eating at the table.   How? Where? When?

They finished their homework in silence.   How? Where? When?

She greeted her relations with a big hug.   How? Where? When?

The scruffy brown dog barked for a long time.   How? Where? When?

The hedgehog built its nest among the leaves.   How? Where? When?

We will do the parachute jump after breakfast.   How? Where? When?

Milly and Zeena built a sandcastle on the beach.   How? Where? When?

Now choose one of the sentences and write it on the sentence wall. Remember to put the prepositional phrase underneath the verb, as it is acting as an adverb.

subject

verb

object

transitive / intransitive

55

 **‹sure›**

sure
_____

unsure
_____ _____

ensure
_____ _____

assure
_____ _____

measure
_____ _____

insure
_____ _____

reassure
_____ _____ _____

pressure
_____ _____

closure
_____ _____

censure
_____ _____

fissure
_____ _____

leisurely
_____ _____ _____

composure
_____ _____ _____

enclosure
_____ _____ _____

overexposure
_____ ___ _____ _____

disclosure
_____ _____ _____

displeasure
_____ _____ _____

countermeasure
_____ _____ _____

Which words from the spelling list complete these sentences?

The chauffeur must _____ that the car is safe to drive.

You need to _____ the dimensions of the box in centimeters.

Are you _____ the location of the mansion is in this direction?

If you are _____ about any information in the brochure, just ask.

The technicians _____ us that the experiment will work.

After the collision, it cost the electrician a lot of money to _____ his van.

Was there a lot of discussion about the_____ of the supermarket?

I was worried about having the operation, but my physician _____d me.

The disturbance of the earthquake created a large, deep _____ in the rock.

The chef at the chateau was under a lot of _____ to cook a superb dinner.

The elderly couple went for a _____ stroll around the village.

The politicians were _____d for the mistakes they made during the emergency.

Find the three words from the spelling list that begin with these prefixes.

‹un-› _____

‹re-› _____

‹dis-› _____

Dictation: ‹sure›

1. _____

_____

2. _____

_____

3. _____

_____

Underline each preposition in green and add a noun phrase to it to make a prepositional phrase.

by _____   up _____

with _____   near _____

down _____   into _____

over _____   until _____

after _____   beneath _____

opposite _____   behind _____

Write a sentence using one of the prepositional phrases above as an adverb. The phrase should tell you more about **how**, **where**, or **when** the verb is happening.

_____

_____

The kind policeman had reassured the old couple during his visit.

subject	verb	object
	transitive / intransitive	

| | (_____) | |

57

Phrasal Verbs

A phrasal verb consists of a verb and one or more other words, usually a preposition or adverb. Put together, these words make a new verb with a new meaning. Can you find the phrasal verbs in these sentences and underline them in red?

My washing machine broke down on Tuesday.

The farmer took off his muddy boots.

What time do you get up in the morning?

Did he throw away those old travel brochures?

Anne tried on the green chiffon ballgown.

I fell over in the park and grazed my knee.

The chauffeur brings back the car every evening.

A fire broke out yesterday in the chef's kitchen.

Use each of these phrasal verbs in a sentence to show its meaning.

cheer up _____

_____

find out _____

_____

turn off _____

_____

come across _____

_____

look forward to _____

_____

Write the meaning for each of the spelling words listed below.

mixture _____
_____

gesture _____
_____

nurture _____
_____

culture _____
_____

venture _____
_____

future _____
_____

agriculture _____
_____

caricature _____
_____

miniature _____
_____

furniture _____
_____

signature _____
_____

architecture _____
_____

‹ture›

mixture

gesture

nurture

culture

venture

future

structure

dentures

fracture

departure

temperature

literature

agriculture

caricature

miniature

furniture

signature

architecture

59

Dictation: ‹ture›

1. _____
   _____

2. _____
   _____

3. _____
   _____

In each sentence, underline the verb in red and identify the subject and the object, if there is one. Then decide whether the verb is transitive or intransitive.

The class measured the triangles accurately. transitive / intransitive

The lions lounged lazily in their enclosure. transitive / intransitive

I will crochet more often in the future. transitive / intransitive

The gallery has some lovely miniature portraits. transitive / intransitive

My grandpa needs new dentures. transitive / intransitive

Ice will melt in hot temperatures. transitive / intransitive

He had fractured his leg in several places. transitive / intransitive

The courageous sailors ventured into the storm. transitive / intransitive

The baker will stir the cake mixture for a long time.

subject	verb	object
	transitive / intransitive	
	(_____)	

More Phrasal Verbs

Which of these phrasal verbs match the descriptions below? Circle the correct phrasal verb for each description.

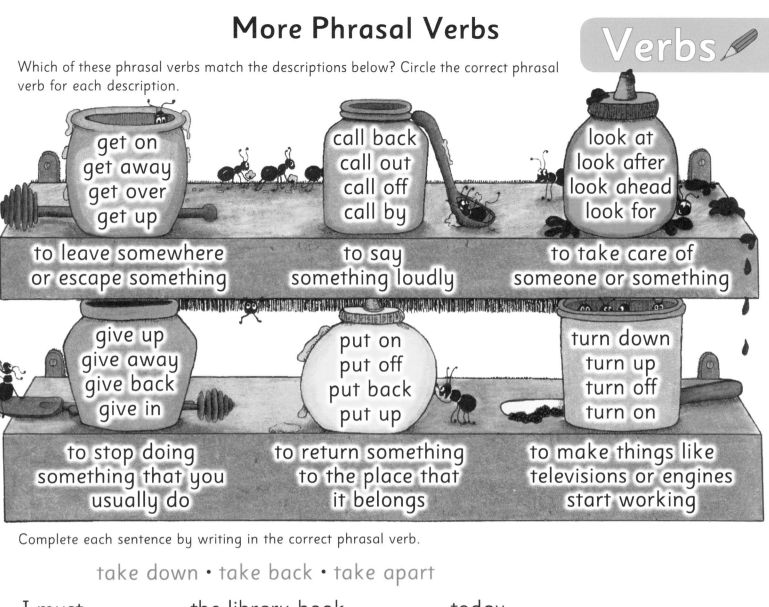

get on
get away
get over
get up

to leave somewhere or escape something

call back
call out
call off
call by

to say something loudly

look at
look after
look ahead
look for

to take care of someone or something

give up
give away
give back
give in

to stop doing something that you usually do

put on
put off
put back
put up

to return something to the place that it belongs

turn down
turn up
turn off
turn on

to make things like televisions or engines start working

Complete each sentence by writing in the correct phrasal verb.

take down • take back • take apart

I must _____ the library book _____ today.

break out • break up • break into

How did the jewel thieves _____ the chateau?

pick up • pick on • pick over

Can you _____ your coat _____, please?

run out of • run away from • run after

Have we _____ milk and sugar yet?

drop by • drop off • drop out

Dad will _____ us _____ on the way home.

check out • check on • check in

Please _____ two hours before your flight to Australia.

‹-ible›

terrible

_____

sensible

_____

edible

_____

horrible

_____

possible

_____

flexible

_____

illegible

_____

audible

_____

tangible

_____

convertible

_____

visible

_____

incredible

_____

feasible

_____

reversible

_____

intelligible

_____

indestructible

_____

irresponsible

_____

comprehensible

_____

Write twelve noun phrases using a different noun and spelling list adjective each time.

Draw a picture to illustrate one of the noun phrases.

62

Dictation: ‹-ible›

1. _____

_____

2. _____

_____

3. _____

_____

Add the prefix to the spelling word to make a new word. How has it changed the meaning?

in + edible

_____

im + possible

_____

in + visible

_____

in + audible

_____

un + intelligible

_____

ir + reversible

_____

in + comprehensible

_____

Remove the prefix from the spelling word to make a new word. How has it changed the meaning?

illegible

_____

indestructible

_____

incredible

_____

irresponsible

_____

The inedible soup had a horrible taste and smell.

subject	verb	object
		and
	transitive / intransitive	

Making Nouns and Adjectives into Verbs

"Grow" the root word on each leaf to make a verb from the same word family. Do this by adding ‹-ate›, ‹-ise/-ize›, or ‹-ify› and then write the verb in the crossword.

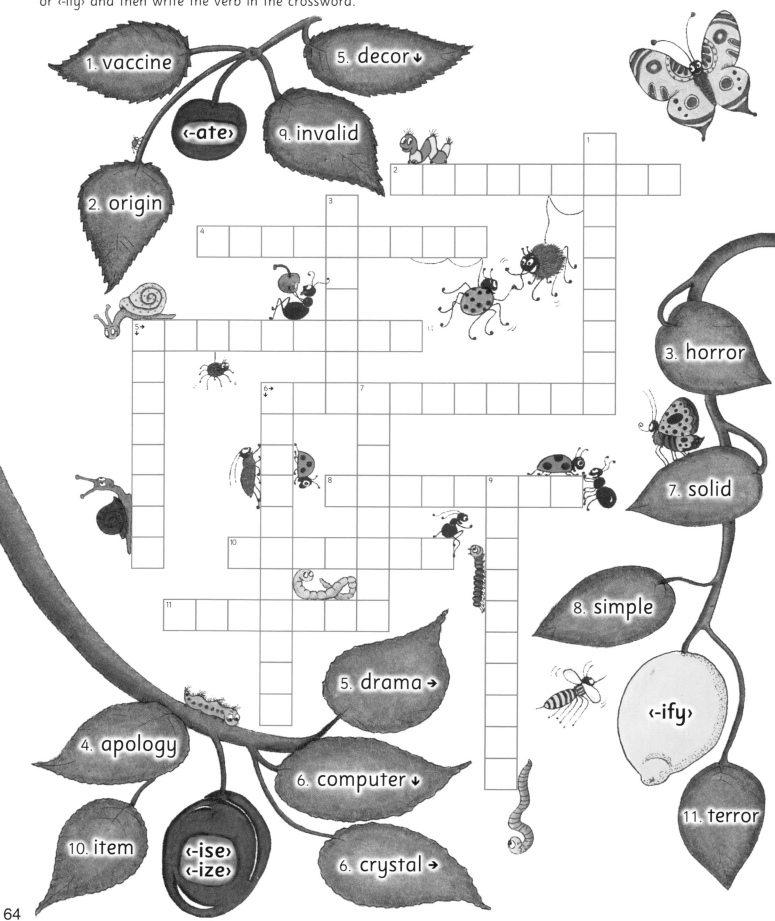

1. vaccine

5. decor ↓

‹-ate›

9. invalid

2. origin

3. horror

7. solid

8. simple

‹-ify›

5. drama →

4. apology

6. computer ↓

11. terror

10. item

‹-ise›
‹-ize›

6. crystal →

64

Which words in the spelling list belong to the same word family as these words?

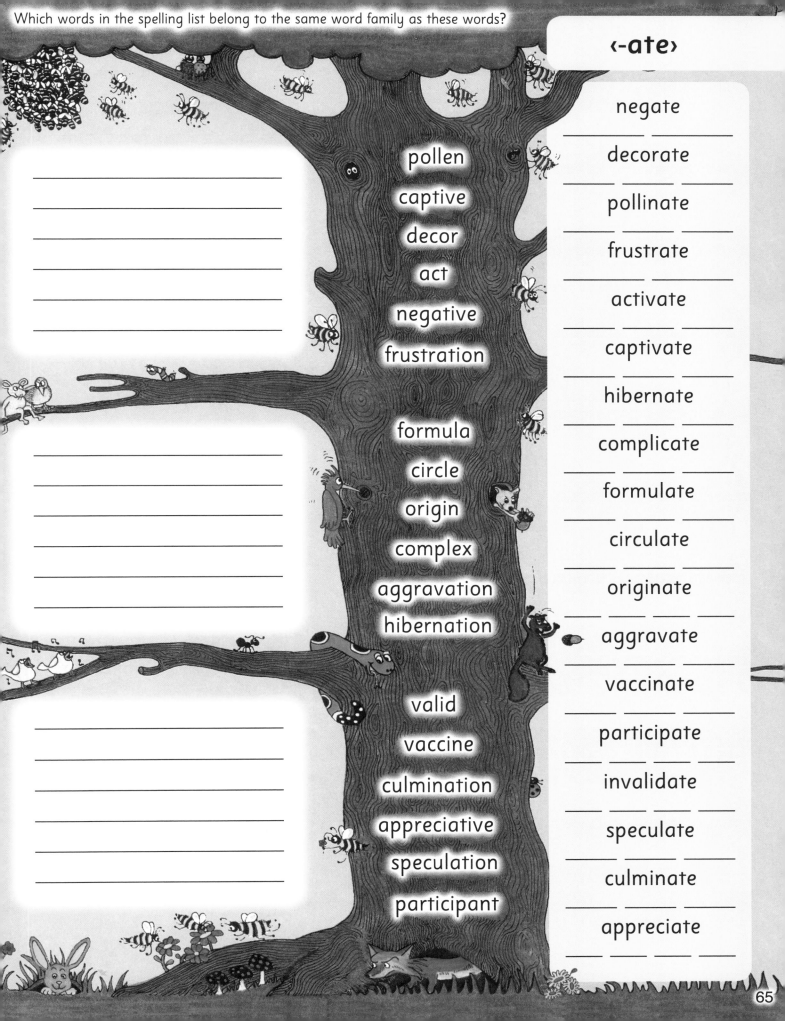

pollen
captive
decor
act
negative
frustration

formula
circle
origin
complex
aggravation
hibernation

valid
vaccine
culmination
appreciative
speculation
participant

‹-ate›

negate
_____ _____
decorate
_____ _____
pollinate
_____ _____
frustrate
_____ _____
activate
_____ _____
captivate
_____ _____
hibernate
_____ _____
complicate
_____ _____
formulate
_____ _____
circulate
_____ _____
originate
_____ _____
aggravate
_____ _____
vaccinate
_____ _____
participate
_____ _____
invalidate
_____ _____
speculate
_____ _____
culminate
_____ _____
appreciate
_____ _____

Dictation: ‹-ate›

1. _____

   _____

2. _____

   _____

3. _____

   _____

Find out what this word means and see how many other words you can make with its letters.

d i s c o m b o b u l a t e

Ben and Gemma have decorated their pictures with stickers.

subject	verb	object
_____ and _____		
	transitive / intransitive	
	(_____)	

Nouns or Verbs? ‹-ce› ‹-se› ‹-cy› ‹-sy›

Add the missing letters to the nouns and verbs. Then complete each sentence by writing in the correct word.

Noun advi __ __   **Verb** advi __ __

We strongly _____ tourists to have travel insurance.

My dad gave me some sensible _____ about the future.

Noun devi __ __   **Verb** devi __ __

Electrical _____s, such as vacuum cleaners and toasters,

are used in many homes.

How did he _____ such a clever plan?

Noun practi __ __   **Verb** practi __ __

I must _____ the piano every day after school.

They have football _____ every Wednesday afternoon.

Noun licen __ __   **Verb** licen __ __

The driver showed his _____ to the police officer.

Every year, they _____ many pilots to fly planes.

Noun prophe __ __   **Verb** prophe __ __

In ancient Greece, people believed that priests had the gift of

_____.

The king asked them to _____ who would win the battle.

device

devise

advice · advise

prophecy

prophesy

license

practice

67

‹-ise› ‹-ize›

prize

_____

capsize

_____

arise

_____

devise

_____

advise

_____

revise

_____

advertise

_____

comprise

_____

despise

_____

disguise

_____

improvise

_____

surmise

_____

surprise

_____

televise

_____

exercise

_____

compromise

_____

enfranchise

_____

disenfranchise

_____

Match the words in the spelling list to the descriptions below.

to make a boat turn over in the water

_____

to tell someone what you think they should do

_____

to get out of bed, stand up, or begin to happen

_____

to invent or plan a way of doing something

_____

to value someone or something very highly

_____

to correct, improve, or add new information

_____

to dislike something and have no respect for it

_____

to change something so it cannot be recognized

_____

to tell people about something in order to sell it

_____

to do something without any time to prepare

_____

to consist of different parts, or to be one part

_____

to guess that something is true

_____

to broadcast something on television

_____

to give people the right to vote

_____

to take away people's right to vote

_____

to do physical activities to stay fit and healthy

_____

to shock or astonish someone in a mild way

_____

to make fewer demands so a problem can be solved

_____

Dictation: ‹-ise› ‹-ize›

1. _____

_____

2. _____

_____

3. _____

_____

In each sentence, which preposition begins a prepositional phrase and which is part of a phrasal verb? Put a green box around all the words in the phrase and underline all the parts of the verb in red. Then write the meaning of the phrasal verb.

The old tree <u>fell down</u> in the night.

To fall down means to fall to the ground.

The spy put on his disguise during the mission.

_____

We will dress up for Tom's surprise party.

_____

My brother normally works out at the gym.

_____

They will go back home after their trip.

_____

The smaller cargo ship capsized after the collision.

subject	verb	object
	transitive / intransitive	
	(_____)	

The Order of Adjectives

When we use more than one adjective in front of a noun, we tend to write them in a certain order. Make a list for each type of adjective in the table below.

1st Determiners	2nd Opinion	3rd Size and Shape	4th Condition and Age	5th Color and Pattern	6th Origin (such as nationality and religion)	7th Material

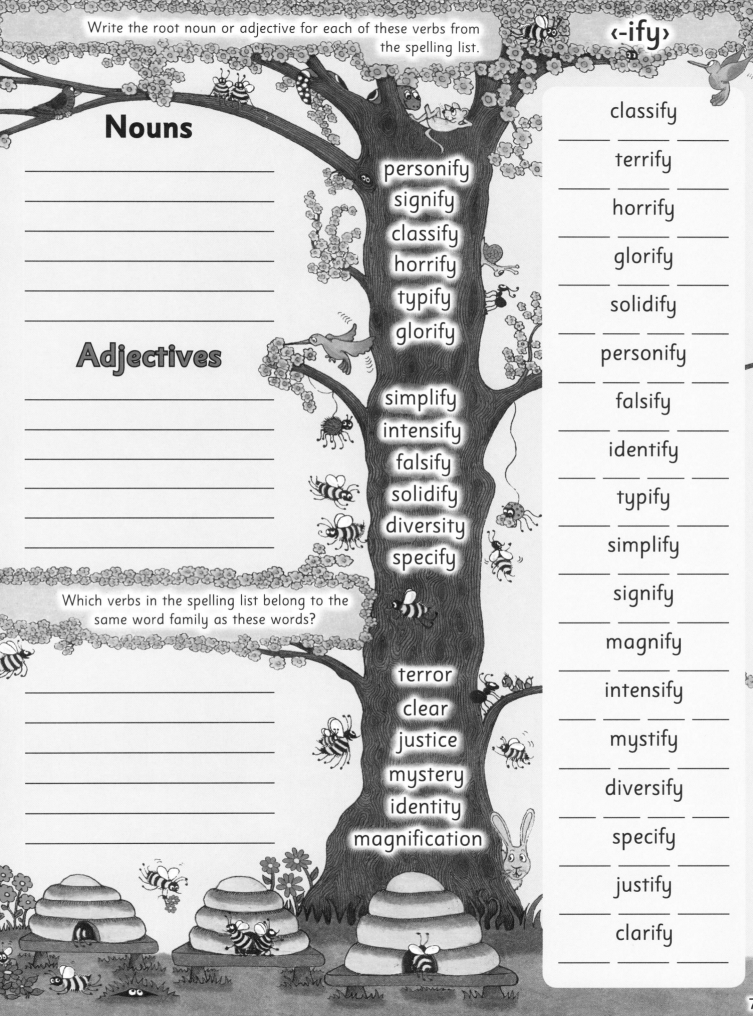

Write the root noun or adjective for each of these verbs from the spelling list.

‹-ify›

Nouns

_____
_____
_____
_____
_____

Adjectives

_____
_____
_____
_____
_____

Which verbs in the spelling list belong to the same word family as these words?

_____
_____
_____
_____

personify
signify
classify
horrify
typify
glorify

simplify
intensify
falsify
solidify
diversity
specify

terror
clear
justice
mystery
identity
magnification

classify ___ ___ ___

terrify ___ ___ ___

horrify ___ ___ ___

glorify ___ ___ ___

solidify ___ ___ ___

personify ___ ___ ___

falsify ___ ___ ___

identify ___ ___ ___

typify ___ ___ ___

simplify ___ ___ ___

signify ___ ___ ___

magnify ___ ___ ___

intensify ___ ___ ___

mystify ___ ___ ___

diversify ___ ___ ___

specify ___ ___ ___

justify ___ ___ ___

clarify ___ ___ ___

Dictation: ‹-ify›

1. _____

_____

2. _____

_____

3. _____

_____

Conjugate the verb "to qualify" in the simple, continuous, and perfect tenses.

	Past	Present	Future
I	_____	qualify	_____
you	_____	_____	_____
he / she / it	_____	_____	_____
we	_____	_____	_____
you	_____	_____	_____
they	_____	_____	_____
I	_____	am qualifying	_____
you	_____	_____	_____
he / she / it	_____	_____	_____
we	_____	_____	_____
you	_____	_____	_____
they	_____	_____	_____
I	_____	have qualified	_____
you	_____	_____	_____
he / she / it	_____	_____	_____
we	_____	_____	_____
you	_____	_____	_____
they	_____	_____	_____

The scary story terrified my brother and sister at bedtime.

subject	verb	object
		—and—
	transitive / intransitive	
	(_____)	

72

Writing Adjectives in the Correct Order

Are these noun phrases correct? If not, rewrite them, putting the adjectives in a better order.

the English beautiful old mansion

_____

some cardboard brown large dented boxes

_____

his striped new silk handsome tie

_____

three strange tall ancient stone megaliths

_____

Think of some adjectives to describe each noun below and put them into a noun phrase. Remember to put the adjectives in the correct order.

parachute

_____

cottage

_____

wreckage

_____

fence

_____

musician

_____

| 1st Determiners | 2nd Opinion | 3rd Size and Shape | 4th Condition and Age | 5th Color and Pattern | 6th Origin | 7th Material |

‹-ous›

famous

nervous

enormous

numerous

generous

vigorous

dangerous

continuous

ridiculous

poisonous

jealous

fabulous

outrageous

hazardous

disastrous

spontaneous

simultaneous

anonymous

famous _____

_____

nervous _____

_____

enormous _____

_____

numerous _____

_____

generous _____

_____

vigorous _____

_____

outrageous _____

_____

hazardous _____

_____

disastrous _____

_____

spontaneous _____

_____

simultaneous _____

_____

anonymous _____

_____

Dictation: ‹-ous›

1. _____

_____

2. _____

_____

3. _____

_____

Complete these noun phrases, using at least three adjectives in each one. Try to use different words each time and remember to put them in the right order.

The _____ mixture

His _____ mustache

A _____ chandelier

Grandma's _____ furniture

The _____ chateau

Her _____ signature

A _____ machine

My _____ prize

| 1st Determiners | 2nd Opinion | 3rd Size and Shape | 4th Condition and Age | 5th Color and Pattern | 6th Origin | 7th Material |

The enormous turnip had grown vigorously over the summer.

subject

verb

object

transitive / intransitive

(_____)

75

Adverbs

Adverbs of Manner

He had disguised himself....   **badly carefully cleverly deliberately**

_____

_____

They asked...   **angrily calmly politely relentlessly**

_____

_____

He was watching...   **anxiously excitedly closely eagerly**

_____

_____

The fox crept...   **cautiously silently stealthily secretly**

_____

_____

I walked...   **quickly lazily carelessly boldly**

_____

_____

The children were eating...   **greedily messily noisily happily**

_____

_____

Which words from the spelling list complete these sentences?

When the ship capsized, the captain was not just angry, he was absolutely _____.

It is never _____ how a successful magician does his tricks.

The audience cheered more loudly tonight than during the _____ performances.

The patient is in a _____ condition because of the infection.

Diamonds and rubies are called _____ jewels because they are rare and valuable.

The mansion had a _____ entrance hall with an enormous chandelier.

The dietician showed us how to make healthy meals that are also _____.

Tom's parents told the pediatrician how _____ they felt about his health.

People are sometimes _____ of strangers.

In the future, I would like to win many _____ awards for my architecture.

A _____ disease can be passed from one person to another by touch.

The autograph did not look real, so the collector was _____ about buying it.

Write a noun phrase with the adjective "mysterious" in it on the lines below. Then draw a picture to illustrate the noun phrase.

<-ious>

serious
_____
various
_____
previous
_____
obvious
_____
curious
_____
furious
_____
anxious
_____
delicious
_____
ferocious
_____
gracious
_____
precious
_____
spacious
_____
dubious
_____
suspicious
_____
mysterious
_____
prestigious
_____
contagious
_____
vicious
_____

Dictation: ‹-ious›

1. _____

_____

2. _____

_____

3. _____

_____

The suffixes ‹-ous› and ‹-ious› are found in adjectives meaning "full of the root word."
Which adjectives match these descriptions?

full of nerves _____   full of anxiety _____

full of space _____   full of mystery _____

full of fury _____   full of disaster _____

full of poison _____   full of curiosity _____

full of vigor _____   full of hazards _____

full of danger _____   full of jealousy _____

full of variety _____   full of suspicion _____

The fabulous chandelier has disappeared in suspicious circumstances.

subject   verb   object

transitive / intransitive

(_____

_____)

78

Adverbs of Degree and Place

Adverbs of degree tell us more about **how much**, or **to what extent**, something is done. In the sentences below, underline the verbs in red and the adverbs in orange. Then write each adverb on the line.

She has almost finished her homework.
To what extent has she finished her homework?   _____

They love their children deeply.
How much do they love their children?   _____

We have hardly eaten anything.
To what extent have we eaten anything?   _____

The boy nearly cut his finger.
To what extent did he cut his finger?   _____

He completely forgot his wife's birthday.
To what extent did he forget her birthday?   _____

Adverbs of place tell us more about **where** something is done. In the sentences below, underline the verbs and adverbs in the appropriate colors, and write each adverb on the line.

The elderly couple live downstairs.
Where do the couple live?   _____

The dog ran indoors.
Where did the dog run?   _____

Our friends were standing nearby.
Where were our friends standing?   _____

The startled bird flew away.
Where did the startled bird fly?   _____

I looked everywhere for my car keys.
Where did I look for my car keys?   _____

‹tious›

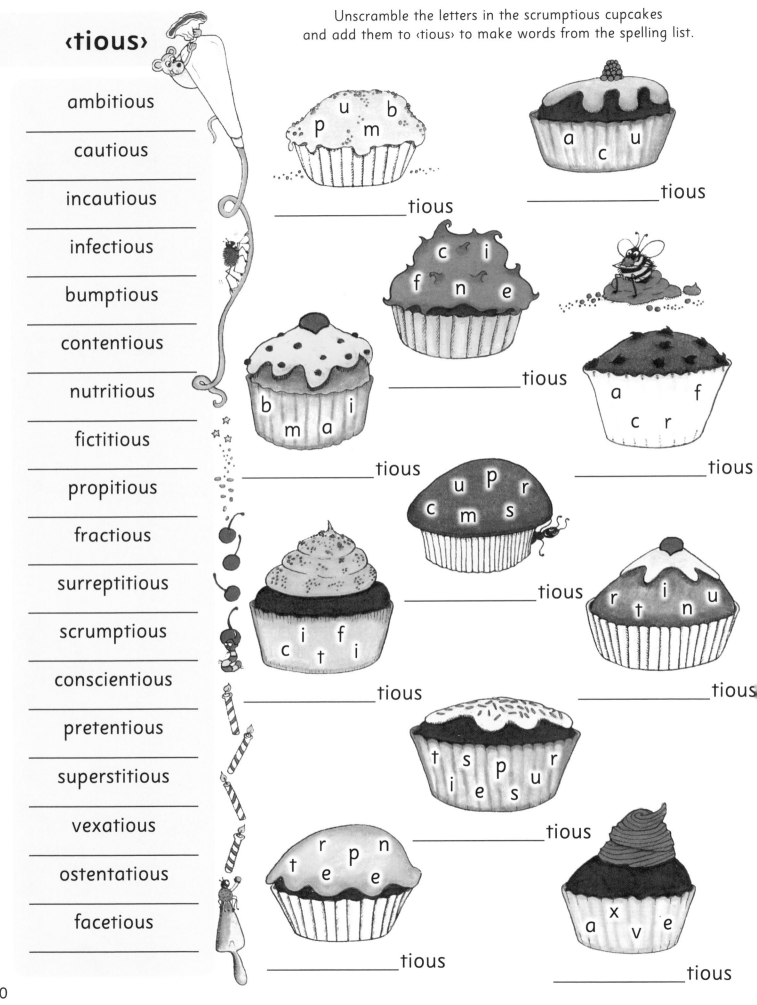

Unscramble the letters in the scrumptious cupcakes
and add them to ‹tious› to make words from the spelling list.

ambitious

cautious

incautious

infectious

bumptious

contentious

nutritious

fictitious

propitious

fractious

surreptitious

scrumptious

conscientious

pretentious

superstitious

vexatious

ostentatious

facetious

_____tious

_____tious

_____tious

_____tious

_____tious

_____tious

_____tious

_____tious

_____tious

_____tious

_____tious

80

Dictation: ‹tious›

1. _____
   _____
2. _____
   _____
3. _____
   _____

Sort these words into adverbs of manner (**how?**), degree (**how much?**), and place (**where?**).

cleverly   almost   indoors   nearby   calmly   hardly

Adverbs of **Manner**	Adverbs of **Degree**	Adverbs of **Place**

quite   abroad   lazily   very   silently   upstairs

The cricket umpire had unfortunately made a contentious decision.

subject

verb

object

transitive / intransitive

Adverbs of Time and Frequency

Adverbs of time and frequency tell us more about **when** or **how often** something is done. In the sentences below, underline the verbs in red and the adverbs in orange. Then write each adverb on the line.

Dad goes to the library occasionally.
How often does Dad go to the library? _____

His boat capsized recently.
When did his boat capsize? _____

He trimmed his mustache regularly.
How often did he trim his mustache? _____

The patient needs an operation soon.
When does the patient need an operation? _____

I am exercising now.
When am I exercising? _____

They meet weekly for band practice.
How often do they meet for band practice? _____

Previously, she had fractured her elbow.
When did she fracture her elbow? _____

Remember that prepositional phrases can act as adverbs. Identify the verb in each sentence and underline it in red. Then write the prepositional phrase that is describing the verb on the line.

Bears hibernate in the winter.
When do bears hibernate? _____

Measure the sugar before the flour.
When should you measure the sugar? _____

Mysterious noises terrified them throughout the night.
When did the mysterious noises terrify them? _____

Write twelve noun phrases using a different noun and spelling list adjective each time.

Draw a picture to illustrate one of the noun phrases.

‹cial›

special

social

crucial

racial

facial

glacial

official

artificial

beneficial

financial

antisocial

commercial

unofficial

superficial

sacrificial

judicial

provincial

controversial

Dictation: ‹cial›

1. _____

   _____

2. _____

   _____

3. _____

   _____

Write the adjective and adverb for each of these root words, choosing the correct suffix/ending.

	Adjective ‹-ous› ‹-ious› ‹tious› ‹cial›	Adverb ‹-ly›
office	_____	_____
danger	_____	_____
caution	_____	_____
nerves	_____	_____
benefit	_____	_____
disaster	_____	_____
ambition	_____	_____
anxiety	_____	_____
finance	_____	_____
suspicion	_____	_____

The famous artist recently painted a controversial portrait.

subject

verb

object

transitive / intransitive

84

Adverbs Describing Other Adverbs

Parse each sentence and write it on the wall. Put both adverbs in the box under the verb, but put the main adverb first and the adverb describing it underneath, and join them with a diagonal line.

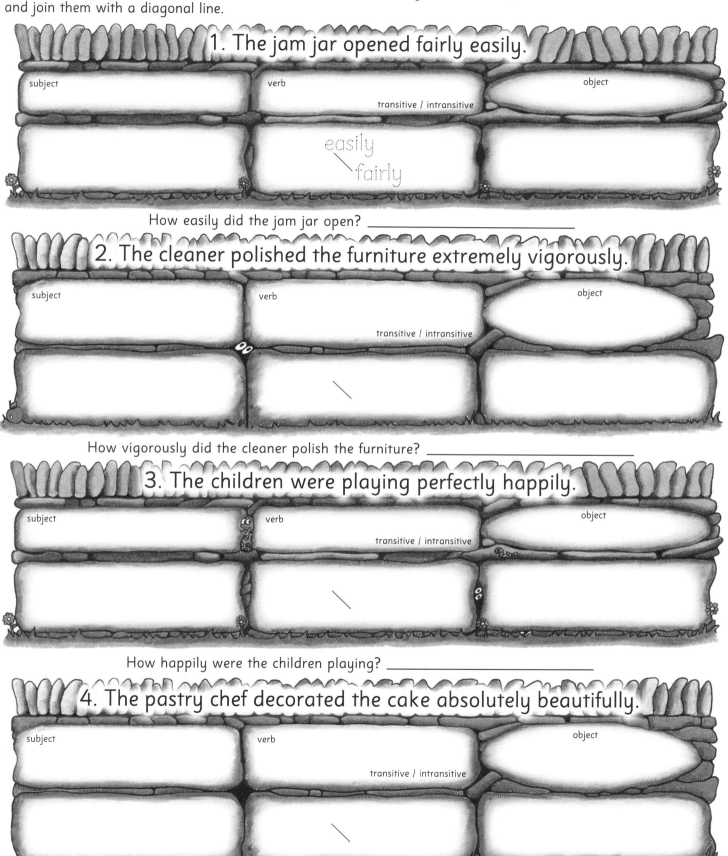

1. The jam jar opened fairly easily.

subject	verb	object
	transitive / intransitive	
	easily / *fairly*	

How easily did the jam jar open? _____

2. The cleaner polished the furniture extremely vigorously.

subject	verb	object
	transitive / intransitive	

How vigorously did the cleaner polish the furniture? _____

3. The children were playing perfectly happily.

subject	verb	object
	transitive / intransitive	

How happily were the children playing? _____

4. The pastry chef decorated the cake absolutely beautifully.

subject	verb	object
	transitive / intransitive	

How beautifully did the pastry chef decorate the cake? _____

Unscramble the letters in the palaces and add them to ‹tial› to make words from the spelling list.

essential

potential

initial

partial

martial

impartial

substantial

confidential

presidential

residential

palatial

torrential

spatial

influential

sequential

preferential

insubstantial

inconsequential

_____tial

_____tial

_____tial

_____tial

_____tial

_____tial

_____tial

_____tial

_____tial

_____tial

Dictation: ‹tial›

1. _____

_____

2. _____

_____

3. _____

_____

Complete the adjectives by adding ‹cial›, ‹sial›, or ‹tial›. Remember that ‹cial› usually follows a vowel letter and ‹tial› normally follows a consonant. Then add ‹-ly› to each word to make an adverb.

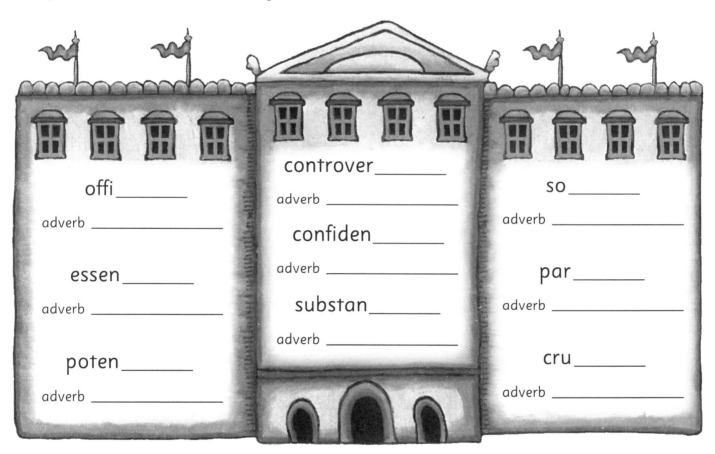

offi_____

adverb _____

essen_____

adverb _____

poten_____

adverb _____

controver_____

adverb _____

confiden_____

adverb _____

substan_____

adverb _____

so_____

adverb _____

par_____

adverb _____

cru_____

adverb _____

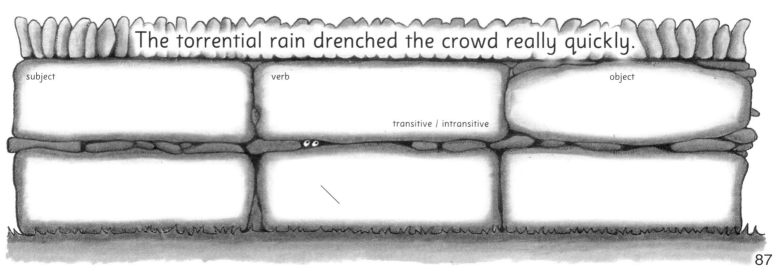

The torrential rain drenched the crowd really quickly.

subject	verb	object
	transitive / intransitive	

87

Adverbs Describing Adjectives

Adverbs can describe verbs, other adverbs, and adjectives. Parse the sentences below, underlining the words in the appropriate colors. Then write the sentence again underneath, adding in the adverb(s) to describe the adjective(s).

The chairs were hard.   **uncomfortably**

_____

_____

I am curious about the surprise.   **quite**

_____

_____

The cheese had a strong smell.   **unusually**

_____

_____

The cakes from the bakery are delicious.   **always**

_____

_____

Her grandmother's ring was expensive.   **really**

_____

_____

The prize for the winner is unusual.   **rather**

_____

_____

She has become a beautiful woman.   **extremely**

_____

_____

The way through the mountains will be dangerous.   **very**

_____

_____

The fragrant flowers had grown tall.   **powerfully exceedingly**

_____

_____

Write the meaning for each of the spelling words listed below.

taxi _____

_____

kiwi _____

_____

ski _____

_____

deli _____

_____

yeti _____

_____

koi _____

_____

spaghetti _____

broccoli _____

_____

origami _____

_____

tsunami _____

_____

pepperoni _____

_____

paparazzi _____

_____

〈-i〉

taxi
_____

kiwi
_____

ski
_____

deli
_____

yeti
_____

koi
_____

bikini
_____

salami
_____

alibi
_____

bonsai
_____

graffiti
_____

safari
_____

spaghetti
_____

broccoli
_____

origami
_____

tsunami
_____

pepperoni
_____

paparazzi
_____

Dictation: ‹-i›

1. _____

_____

2. _____

_____

3. _____

_____

Find the adverb in each sentence and underline it in orange. Then decide whether it is an adverb of manner (**how?**), degree (**how much?**), place (**where?**), time (**when?**), or frequency (**how often?**).

I have just finished the book.　manner · degree · place · time · frequency

Can you meet me there?　manner · degree · place · time · frequency

We will be sitting outside.　manner · degree · place · time · frequency

It will be cloudy later.　manner · degree · place · time · frequency

He really loved to sing.　manner · degree · place · time · frequency

We are leaving tomorrow.　manner · degree · place · time · frequency

The man laughed nervously.　manner · degree · place · time · frequency

She always swims on Tuesdays.　manner · degree · place · time · frequency

The boys were grinning cheekily.　manner · degree · place · time · frequency

They frequently visit the library.　manner · degree · place · time · frequency

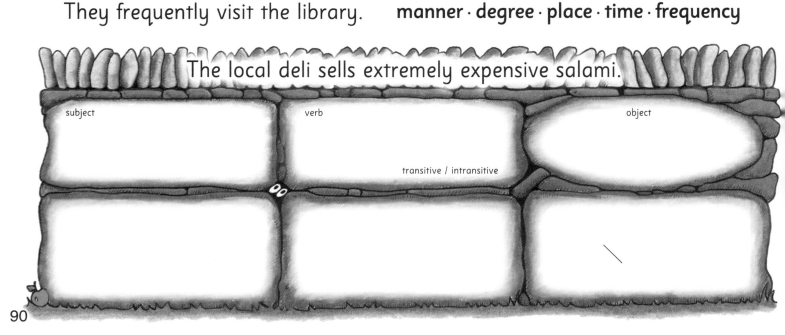

The local deli sells extremely expensive salami.

subject　　verb　　object

transitive / intransitive

90

Irregular Plurals: ‹-i›

Many nouns in English that end in ‹-us› have a Latin origin. Most of these have a regular plural, but some make the plural in the Latin way, replacing ‹-us› with ‹-i›. Make these words plural and look them up in a dictionary to find out their meanings.

stimulus_____   nucleus_____   alumnus_____

Some nouns ending in ‹-us› come from Greek rather than Latin. Most nouns with a Greek or Latin origin form their plurals in the usual way by adding ‹-es›. Turn these singular nouns into plural ones.

octopus_____   platypus_____   virus_____

Some nouns can be made in either way, by adding ‹-es› or replacing ‹-us› with ‹-i›. Rewrite these sentences so that the noun in bold is plural and make sure everything else agrees. Then draw several pictures of each item to match.

A **hippopotamus** wallows in mud to stay cool.

_____

I have a **cactus** in a pot on my windowsill.

_____

A **crocus** is a small flower that grows in the spring.

_____

A mushroom is a **fungus** that is often edible.

_____

‹graph›

graph

graphic

digraph

telegraph

paragraph

polygraph

autograph

photograph

biography

geography

calligraphy

cartographer

homograph

graphically

bibliography

lexicography

choreography

autobiography

Unscramble the letters in the graphs and charts and add them to ‹graph› to make words from the spelling list.

_____ graph

_____ graph

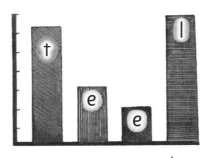
_____ graph

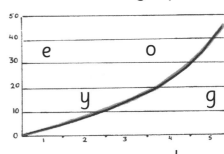
_____ graph ___

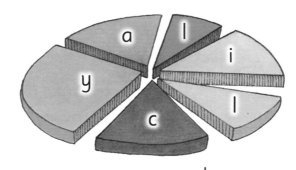
_____ graph ___

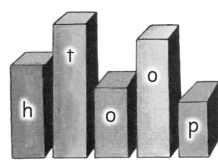
_____ graph

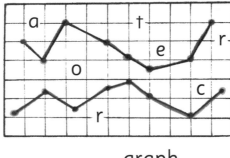
_____ graph ___

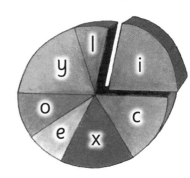
_____ graph ___

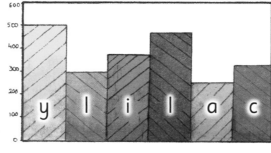
graph _____

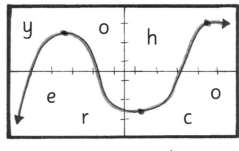
_____ graph ___

92

Dictation: ‹graph›

1. _____
   _____

2. _____
   _____

3. _____
   _____

Write the plural for each of these words.

doorway _____ princess _____

ditch _____ cactus _____

woman _____ diary _____

potato _____ crash _____

hoax _____ nucleus _____

pie _____ person _____

kilo _____ knife _____

mouse _____ gallery _____

octopus _____ cowboy _____

life _____ sheep _____

The cartographer decorated his map with beautiful calligraphy.

subject

verb

object

transitive / intransitive

93

Using a Colon and Bullet Points in a List

Instead of commas, we can use bullet points to separate the items in a list. Make five lists in this way. Say what each one is about at the top and put a colon after the last word to indicate a pause. Then write each item in the list on a separate line, starting with a bullet point.

The names of the people in my family are:

-
-
-
-
-
-

Match the words in the spelling list to the descriptions below.

‹-ology›

the scientific study of plants, animals, and all living things

_____

the scientific study of animals and how they behave

_____

the scientific study of the rocks and soil that form the Earth, and how they have changed

_____

the scientific study of the relationship between all living things and their environment

_____

the scientific study of birds

_____

the scientific study of the origin and structure of the universe

_____

the study of words, especially their origin, history, and changes of meaning

_____

the scientific study of the way in which people in groups or societies behave

_____

the scientific study of weather conditions and weather forecasting

_____

the scientific study of ancient societies through the buildings, graves, and tools that remain

_____

the study of the language, history, and culture of ancient Egypt

_____

the scientific study of people, their societies, and cultures

_____

biology

_____

geology

_____

ecology

_____

zoology

_____

technology

_____

terminology

_____

ideology

_____

mythology

_____

cosmology

_____

anthology

_____

chronology

_____

ornithology

_____

Egyptology

_____

sociology

_____

etymology

_____

meteorology

_____

anthropology

_____

archaeology

_____

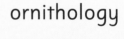

Dictation: ‹-ology›

1. _____

   _____

2. _____

   _____

3. _____

   _____

Make two lists below, using bullet points instead of commas. Remember to say what each one is about at the top and put a colon after the last word to indicate a pause. Then write each item in the list on a separate line, starting with a bullet point.

Modern technology is developing at a rapid rate.

subject	verb	object
	transitive / intransitive	

( )( ) Parentheses (Round Brackets) ( )( )

Decide which piece of extra information (see **a**, **b**, **c**, or **d** below) goes with each sentence and write it in.

I am still reading the anthology _____
that you gave me last year.

Please remember to use paragraphs in your writing. _____
_____

Some people believe the yeti _____
is real, but others think it is a mythical creature.

Koi carp are cold-water fish that prefer temperatures between 15 and
25°C _____ .

     a. (there are over 500 poems!)   **b.** (59–77°F)
  c. (It makes it so much easier to read!)   **d.** (or Abominable Snowman)

Turn each of these long sentences into two shorter sentences. Put the main information in the first one, then rewrite the extra information as a second sentence, without the parentheses.

He is the author of many books on zoology (the scientific study of animals and how they behave).

_____

_____

They are going on an African safari (meaning "journey") to see the lions, giraffes, and hippopotamuses.

_____

_____

This biography is about Samuel Morse (born April 1791), who helped invent the telegraph and Morse code.

_____

_____

Read the paragraph below and put parentheses around the extra pieces of information.

This year, I joined the YOC Young Ornithologists Club to learn more about birds. I'm also learning how to make animals in origami that's the traditional Japanese art of paper folding. Vicky she's my younger sister is doing it too. Here's a photograph of the owl and penguin my favorite! that we made last week. Tonight we're having either a pepperoni, b salami, or c sausage pizza!

‹-ment›

ailment

treatment

element

comment

payment

assortment

agreement

government

argument

astonishment

statement

enjoyment

parliament

entertainment

embarrassment

encouragement

disappointment

discouragement

Write the meaning for each of the spelling words below.

ailment _____

_____

treatment _____

_____

element _____

_____

comment _____

_____

payment _____

_____

assortment _____

_____

parliament _____

_____

entertainment _____

_____

embarrassment _____

_____

encouragement _____

_____

disappointment _____

_____

discouragement _____

_____

Dictation: ‹-ment›

1. _____

_____

2. _____

_____

3. _____

_____

Use a dictionary to find out what this word means and see how many other words you can make with its letters.

a c c o m p l i s h m e n t

The two friends reached an agreement after their argument.

subject	verb	object
	transitive / intransitive	

Homophone Mix-Ups

Write the meanings for these pairs of homophones.
If you are unsure, look them up in the dictionary.

alter

altar

sail

sale

piece

peace

week

weak

hire

higher

medal

meddle

profit

prophet

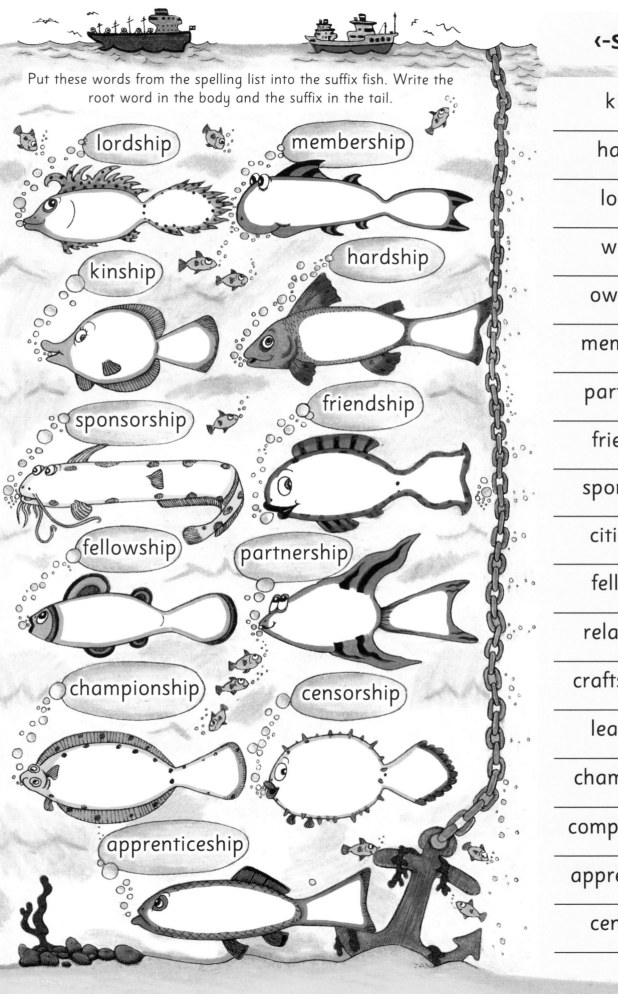

Put these words from the spelling list into the suffix fish. Write the root word in the body and the suffix in the tail.

lordship

membership

hardship

kinship

friendship

sponsorship

fellowship

partnership

championship

censorship

apprenticeship

kinship

hardship

lordship

worship

ownership

membership

partnership

friendship

sponsorship

citizenship

fellowship

relationship

craftsmanship

leadership

championship

companionship

apprenticeship

censorship

Dictation: ‹-ship›

Write the meanings for these pairs of homophones (words that sound the same, but have different spellings and meanings). If you are unsure of a word, look it up in the dictionary.

doe
dough _____

feet _____

feat _____

poor _____

pour _____

wail _____

whale _____

Their long friendship had started in childhood.

subject   verb   object

transitive / intransitive

Homographs and Homonyms

Homographs are words that share the same spelling, but have a different meaning.
Homographs that look and sound the same are called homonyms.

Draw a couple of pictures for each homonym to show two of its different meanings.

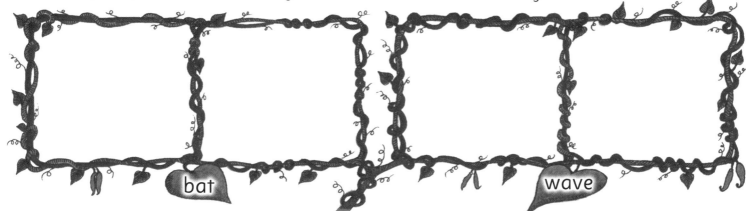

bat

wave

Can you think of a word that can mean both of these things?

a sharp loud sound made by a dog

the tough covering of a tree trunk and its branches

a round object used in sports

a large, formal dance

a dark blue color

a fleet of battleships

in the opposite direction to right

the past tense of the verb "to leave"

to make food or drink go down your throat

a small bird with pointed wings and a long forked tail

the black area in the middle of your eye

what a young schoolchild is sometimes called

a waterbird with short legs and a wide beak

to lower your head quickly to avoid being hit

103

‹-ward›

Write a sentence for each of the spelling words below.

onward
forward
outward
toward
backward
skyward
homeward
downward
wayward
untoward
awkward
afterward
leeward
straightforward
henceforward
windward
southeastward
northwestward

onward _____

_____

forward _____

_____

outward _____

_____

toward _____

_____

backward _____

_____

skyward _____

_____

homeward _____

_____

downward _____

_____

wayward _____

_____

untoward _____

_____

awkward _____

_____

afterward _____

_____

Dictation: ‹-ward›

1. _____
_____

2. _____
_____

3. _____
_____

Write the directions in words on the compass.

_____

N

_____ **NW**   **NE** _____

_____ **W**   **E** _____

_____ **SW**   **SE** _____

S

_____

The ship's captain was steadily sailing a southwestward course.

subject	verb	object
	transitive / intransitive	

Homographs and Heteronyms

Homographs are words that share the same spelling, but have a different meaning.
Homographs that look the same but sound different are called heteronyms.

bow /boa/

/bou/

wind /wind/

/wiend/

close /cloas/

/cloaz/

tear /tair/

/tear/

minute /minit/

/mienuet/

present /prezent/

/prezent/

Look at the pairs of heteronyms and use each word correctly in a sentence.
The pronunciation guide will help you decide which word is which.

_____
_____
_____
_____
_____
_____
_____
_____
_____
_____
_____
_____
_____
_____
_____
_____
_____
_____
_____
_____
_____
_____
_____
_____
_____
_____
_____
_____
_____
_____

Match the words in the spelling list to the descriptions below.

‹sch›

to plan something secretly

_____

an unstressed vowel without its pure sound

_____

a place for teaching and learning

_____

a list of activities and the times they will happen

_____

money given to help pay for someone's education

_____

someone who studies, or has a scholarship

_____

someone whose job is to teach in a school

_____

someone who is plotting, or making secret plans

_____

a fast sailing ship with two or more masts

_____

a very formal word meaning "avoid" or "shun"

_____

to talk in a friendly way, often at a social event

_____

a thin piece of fried meat covered in breadcrumbs

_____

school

scholar

schedule

schwa

scheme

scholarship

schooner

eschew

schmooze

schemer

schnitzel

schoolteacher

kitsch

schmaltz

scherzo

schism

schematic

schizophrenic

Find the words in the spelling list that are related to "school" and write them in the word family tree.

_____

_____

_____

school

107

Dictation: ‹sch›

1. _____
   _____

2. _____
   _____

3. _____
   _____

Write the meanings for these pairs of heteronyms (words that look the same, but sound different and have different meanings). The pronunciation guide will help you decide which word is which.

row   /row/   _____
                       _____

             /rou/   _____
                       _____

wound   /wound/   _____
                       _____

             /woond/   _____
                       _____

object   /**ob**ject/ _____
                       _____

             /ob**ject**/ _____
                       _____

content   /**con**tent/ _____
                       _____

             /con**tent**/ _____
                       _____

The magnificent schooner made its hazardous journey across the ocean.

subject	verb	object
	transitive / intransitive	

Antonyms and Synonyms

Antonyms are words which have the opposite meaning to another word. Write an antonym for each of the words below.

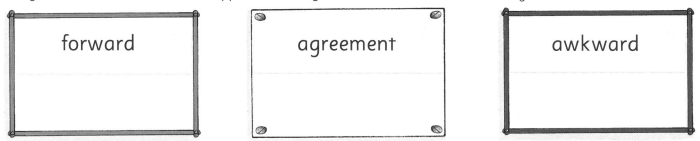

forward

agreement

awkward

Synonyms are words which have the same meaning, or nearly the same meaning, as another word. Write a synonym for each of the words below.

ailment

argument

afterward

Think of some synonyms and antonyms for each of these adjectives and write them in the wooden crate. If you are unsure, use a thesaurus to help you.

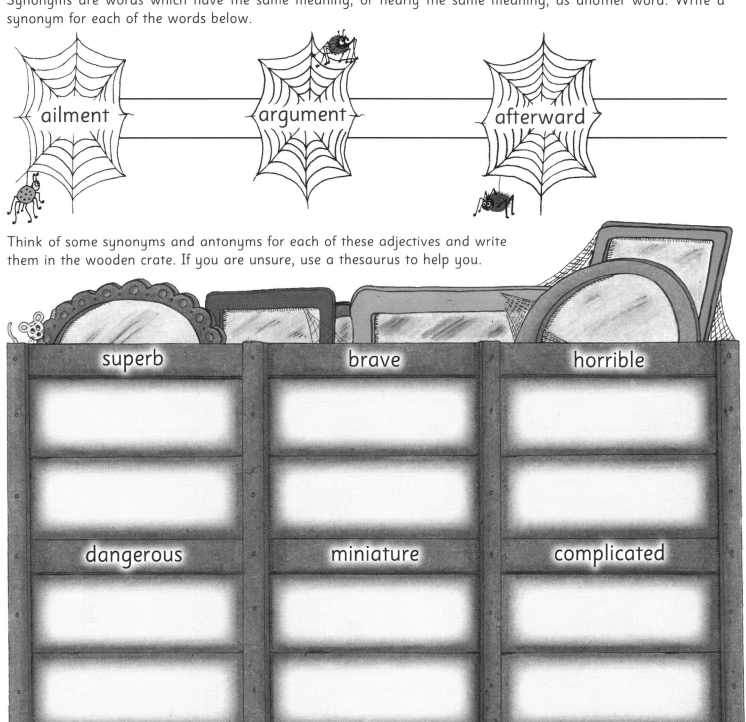

superb

brave

horrible

dangerous

miniature

complicated

Spelling Test 1

1. _____
2. _____
3. _____
4. _____
5. _____
6. _____
7. _____
8. _____
9. _____
10. _____
11. _____
12. _____
13. _____
14. _____
15. _____
16. _____
17. _____
18. _____

Spelling Test 2

1. _____
2. _____
3. _____
4. _____
5. _____
6. _____
7. _____
8. _____
9. _____
10. _____
11. _____
12. _____
13. _____
14. _____
15. _____
16. _____
17. _____
18. _____

Spelling Test 3

1. _____
2. _____
3. _____
4. _____
5. _____
6. _____
7. _____
8. _____
9. _____
10. _____
11. _____
12. _____
13. _____
14. _____
15. _____
16. _____
17. _____
18. _____

Spelling Test 4

1. _____
2. _____
3. _____
4. _____
5. _____
6. _____
7. _____
8. _____
9. _____
10. _____
11. _____
12. _____
13. _____
14. _____
15. _____
16. _____
17. _____
18. _____

Spelling Test 5

1. _____
2. _____
3. _____
4. _____
5. _____
6. _____
7. _____
8. _____
9. _____
10. _____
11. _____
12. _____
13. _____
14. _____
15. _____
16. _____
17. _____
18. _____

Spelling Test 6

1. _____
2. _____
3. _____
4. _____
5. _____
6. _____
7. _____
8. _____
9. _____
10. _____
11. _____
12. _____
13. _____
14. _____
15. _____
16. _____
17. _____
18. _____

Spelling Test 7

1. _____
2. _____
3. _____
4. _____
5. _____
6. _____
7. _____
8. _____
9. _____
10. _____
11. _____
12. _____
13. _____
14. _____
15. _____
16. _____
17. _____
18. _____

Spelling Test 8

1. _____
2. _____
3. _____
4. _____
5. _____
6. _____
7. _____
8. _____
9. _____
10. _____
11. _____
12. _____
13. _____
14. _____
15. _____
16. _____
17. _____
18. _____

Spelling Test 9

1. _____
2. _____
3. _____
4. _____
5. _____
6. _____
7. _____
8. _____
9. _____
10. _____
11. _____
12. _____
13. _____
14. _____
15. _____
16. _____
17. _____
18. _____

Spelling Test 10

1. _____
2. _____
3. _____
4. _____
5. _____
6. _____
7. _____
8. _____
9. _____
10. _____
11. _____
12. _____
13. _____
14. _____
15. _____
16. _____
17. _____
18. _____

Spelling Test 11

1. _____
2. _____
3. _____
4. _____
5. _____
6. _____
7. _____
8. _____
9. _____
10. _____
11. _____
12. _____
13. _____
14. _____
15. _____
16. _____
17. _____
18. _____

Spelling Test 12

1. _____
2. _____
3. _____
4. _____
5. _____
6. _____
7. _____
8. _____
9. _____
10. _____
11. _____
12. _____
13. _____
14. _____
15. _____
16. _____
17. _____
18. _____

Spelling Test 13

1. _____
2. _____
3. _____
4. _____
5. _____
6. _____
7. _____
8. _____
9. _____
10. _____
11. _____
12. _____
13. _____
14. _____
15. _____
16. _____
17. _____
18. _____

Spelling Test 14

1. _____
2. _____
3. _____
4. _____
5. _____
6. _____
7. _____
8. _____
9. _____
10. _____
11. _____
12. _____
13. _____
14. _____
15. _____
16. _____
17. _____
18. _____

Spelling Test 15

1. _____
2. _____
3. _____
4. _____
5. _____
6. _____
7. _____
8. _____
9. _____
10. _____
11. _____
12. _____
13. _____
14. _____
15. _____
16. _____
17. _____
18. _____

Spelling Test 16

1. _____
2. _____
3. _____
4. _____
5. _____
6. _____
7. _____
8. _____
9. _____
10. _____
11. _____
12. _____
13. _____
14. _____
15. _____
16. _____
17. _____
18. _____

Spelling Test 17

1. _____
2. _____
3. _____
4. _____
5. _____
6. _____
7. _____
8. _____
9. _____
10. _____
11. _____
12. _____
13. _____
14. _____
15. _____
16. _____
17. _____
18. _____

Spelling Test 18

1. _____
2. _____
3. _____
4. _____
5. _____
6. _____
7. _____
8. _____
9. _____
10. _____
11. _____
12. _____
13. _____
14. _____
15. _____
16. _____
17. _____
18. _____

Spelling Test 19

1. _____
2. _____
3. _____
4. _____
5. _____
6. _____
7. _____
8. _____
9. _____
10. _____
11. _____
12. _____
13. _____
14. _____
15. _____
16. _____
17. _____
18. _____

Spelling Test 20

1. _____
2. _____
3. _____
4. _____
5. _____
6. _____
7. _____
8. _____
9. _____
10. _____
11. _____
12. _____
13. _____
14. _____
15. _____
16. _____
17. _____
18. _____

Spelling Test 21

1. _____
2. _____
3. _____
4. _____
5. _____
6. _____
7. _____
8. _____
9. _____
10. _____
11. _____
12. _____
13. _____
14. _____
15. _____
16. _____
17. _____
18. _____

Spelling Test 22

1. _____
2. _____
3. _____
4. _____
5. _____
6. _____
7. _____
8. _____
9. _____
10. _____
11. _____
12. _____
13. _____
14. _____
15. _____
16. _____
17. _____
18. _____

Spelling Test 23

1. _____
2. _____
3. _____
4. _____
5. _____
6. _____
7. _____
8. _____
9. _____
10. _____
11. _____
12. _____
13. _____
14. _____
15. _____
16. _____
17. _____
18. _____

Spelling Test 24

1. _____
2. _____
3. _____
4. _____
5. _____
6. _____
7. _____
8. _____
9. _____
10. _____
11. _____
12. _____
13. _____
14. _____
15. _____
16. _____
17. _____
18. _____

Spelling Test 25

1. _____
2. _____
3. _____
4. _____
5. _____
6. _____
7. _____
8. _____
9. _____
10. _____
11. _____
12. _____
13. _____
14. _____
15. _____
16. _____
17. _____
18. _____

Spelling Test 26

1. _____
2. _____
3. _____
4. _____
5. _____
6. _____
7. _____
8. _____
9. _____
10. _____
11. _____
12. _____
13. _____
14. _____
15. _____
16. _____
17. _____
18. _____

Spelling Test 27

1. _____
2. _____
3. _____
4. _____
5. _____
6. _____
7. _____
8. _____
9. _____
10. _____
11. _____
12. _____
13. _____
14. _____
15. _____
16. _____
17. _____
18. _____

Spelling Test 28

1. _____
2. _____
3. _____
4. _____
5. _____
6. _____
7. _____
8. _____
9. _____
10. _____
11. _____
12. _____
13. _____
14. _____
15. _____
16. _____
17. _____
18. _____

Spelling Test 29

1. _____
2. _____
3. _____
4. _____
5. _____
6. _____
7. _____
8. _____
9. _____
10. _____
11. _____
12. _____
13. _____
14. _____
15. _____
16. _____
17. _____
18. _____

Spelling Test 30

1. _____
2. _____
3. _____
4. _____
5. _____
6. _____
7. _____
8. _____
9. _____
10. _____
11. _____
12. _____
13. _____
14. _____
15. _____
16. _____
17. _____
18. _____

Spelling Test 31

1. _____
2. _____
3. _____
4. _____
5. _____
6. _____
7. _____
8. _____
9. _____
10. _____
11. _____
12. _____
13. _____
14. _____
15. _____
16. _____
17. _____
18. _____

Spelling Test 32

1. _____
2. _____
3. _____
4. _____
5. _____
6. _____
7. _____
8. _____
9. _____
10. _____
11. _____
12. _____
13. _____
14. _____
15. _____
16. _____
17. _____
18. _____

Spelling Test 33

1. _____
2. _____
3. _____
4. _____
5. _____
6. _____
7. _____
8. _____
9. _____
10. _____
11. _____
12. _____
13. _____
14. _____
15. _____
16. _____
17. _____
18. _____

Spelling Test 34

1. _____
2. _____
3. _____
4. _____
5. _____
6. _____
7. _____
8. _____
9. _____
10. _____
11. _____
12. _____
13. _____
14. _____
15. _____
16. _____
17. _____
18. _____

Spelling Test 35

1. _____
2. _____
3. _____
4. _____
5. _____
6. _____
7. _____
8. _____
9. _____
10. _____
11. _____
12. _____
13. _____
14. _____
15. _____
16. _____
17. _____
18. _____

Spelling Test 36

1. _____
2. _____
3. _____
4. _____
5. _____
6. _____
7. _____
8. _____
9. _____
10. _____
11. _____
12. _____
13. _____
14. _____
15. _____
16. _____
17. _____
18. _____

Verb Tenses

Write the verbs in each of the tenses in the tense tent.

	Past	Present	Future
Simple		look hug compete identify laugh	
Continuous			
Perfect			